Editor-in-Chief and Founder:
Lyndon H. LaRouche, Jr.
Editorial Board: *Lyndon H. LaRouche, Jr. , Helga Zepp-LaRouche, Paul Gallagher, Tony Papert, Gerald Rose, Dennis Small, Jeffrey Steinberg, William Wertz*
Co-Editors: *Paul Gallagher, Tony Papert*
Managing Editor: *Nancy Spannaus*
Technology: *Marsha Freeman*
Books: *Katherine Notley*
Ebooks: *Richard Burden*
Graphics: *Alan Yue*
Photos: *Stuart Lewis*
Circulation Manager: *Stanley Ezrol*

INTELLIGENCE DIRECTORS
Counterintelligence: *Jeffrey Steinberg, Michele Steinberg*
Economics: *John Hoefle, Marcia Merry Baker, Paul Gallagher*
History: *Anton Chaitkin*
Ibero-America: *Dennis Small*
Russia and Eastern Europe: *Rachel Douglas*
United States: *Debra Freeman*

INTERNATIONAL BUREAUS
Bogotá: *Miriam Redondo*
Berlin: *Rainer Apel*
Copenhagen: *Tom Gillesberg*
Houston: *Harley Schlanger*
Lima: *Sara Madueño*
Melbourne: *Robert Barwick*
Mexico City: *Gerardo Castilleja Chávez*
New Delhi: *Ramtanu Maitra*
Paris: *Christine Bierre*
Stockholm: *Ulf Sandmark*
United Nations, N.Y.C.: *Leni Rubinstein*
Washington, D.C.: *William Jones*
Wiesbaden: *Göran Haglund*

ON THE WEB
e-mail: eirns@larouchepub.com
www.larouchepub.com
www.executiveintelligencereview.com
www.larouchepub.com/eiw
Webmaster: *John Sigerson*
Assistant Webmaster: *George Hollis*
Editor, Arabic-language edition: *Hussein Askary*

EIR (ISSN 0273-6314) *is published weekly (50 issues), by EIR News Service, Inc., P.O. Box 17390, Washington, D.C. 20041-0390. (703) 777-9451*

European Headquarters: E.I.R. GmbH, Postfach Bahnstrasse 9a, D-65205, Wiesbaden, Germany
Tel: 49-611-73650
Homepage: http://www.eirna.com
e-mail: eirna@eirna.com
Director: Georg Neudecker

Montreal, Canada: 514-461-1557

Denmark: EIR - Danmark, Sankt Knuds Vej 11, basement left, DK-1903 Frederiksberg, Denmark. Tel.: +45 35 43 60 40, Fax: +45 35 43 87 57. e-mail: eirdk@hotmail.com.

Mexico City: EIR, Sor Juana Inés de la Cruz 242-2 Col. Agricultura C.P. 11360 Delegación M. Hidalgo, México D.F. Tel. (5525) 5318-2301 eirmexico@gmail.com

Postmaster: Send all address changes to *EIR*, P.O. Box 17390, Washington, D.C. 20041-0390.

Signed articles in *EIR* represent the views of the authors, and not necessarily those of the Editorial Board.

100 Years of Stupidity: The Cesspool That Was the Twentieth Century

ABOUT THIS ISSUE:

Breaking Free, Finally, of the Twentieth Century

We can be from where we seem to be right now into where we have to be, in 18 months or so; under the emergence of a new kind of Presidency—with respect to what happened since the assassination of the leading President, at the beginning of the Twentieth Century.

The Twentieth Century was the take-off point for the destruction of the United States. And the United States has been corrupted increasingly since that time. The Twentieth Century has been the worst fraud propagated on the planet. Because what that represented, the development of the Twentieth Century, at the very *date* of the Twentieth Century, under Hilbert, was the degeneration of the United States. And you had some Presidents who fought against that, *but*, they were disposed of in due course, or summarily, as you may take the choice.

So, we have to have that concept of history. The Twentieth Century—which we're still living in, and we hope to be out of it very soon—has been the doom, which we have suffered as a nation, under the influence of the Twentieth Century; which has been a disaster, an increasing disaster.

And we are in a process where we can change that direction. In order to change that direction, if we can break through the situation in Russia against the operation that's going on in Russia now, against Russia, we have a very good shot at pulling together a new conception of the nations of the planet, henceforth. And with 18 months, we can have that as a reality; because it's not the quantity, it's the quality that counts. What's the quality of the trend, as against what the quantity has been so far. But if we understand that the Twentieth Century was a human disaster, a global disaster, and see the way to solve that problem; give us 18 months of the right course of action, and this planet will be changed in a beautiful way.

—*Lyndon LaRouche*
Editor-in-Chief

EIR Contents

www.larouchepub.com   Volume 42, Number 24, June 12, 2015

**Cover
This Week**

*The assassination
of Archduke
Franz Ferdinand
in Sarajevo, June
28, 1914*

Sarajevo, June 28, 1914

cc/Silver Starre

I. One Hundred Years of Stupidity

**4 Hilbert and Russell: The Suffocation of
Science by Mathematics**
By Phil Rubenstein

**8 The Murder of Music With the Death of
Brahms**
By Mindy Pechenuk

**18 T.H. Huxley's Hideous Revolution in
Science**
By Paul Glumaz

**30 The Ouster of Bismarck and the Start of
World War I**
By Jeffrey Steinberg

**35 London's Murder of McKinley Launched a
Century of Assassinations**
By Jeffrey Steinberg and Anton Chaitkin

**38 The First Sino-Japanese War, 1894-95 & the
Russo-Japanese War, 1904-05**
By William Jones

**41 LaRouche Fireside Chat:
We Have Within Us, The
Power of Victory**

II. Helga Zepp-LaRouche Addresses the Manhattan Project, June 6, 2105

**55 The Promethean
Challenge: BRICS, a
New Era for Mankind**
By Helga Zepp-LaRouche

Hilbert and Russell: The Suffocation Of Science by Mathematics

by Phil Rubinstein

"As a mathematician he was disturbed by a certain lack of order in the triumphs of the physicists."
— *A biographer on David Hilbert*

June 9—The Twentieth Century, into the present early phase of the Twenty-First, has witnessed the near-total destruction of the progress in human self-conception, that occurred from the Fifteenth Century Golden Renaissance to the end of the Nineteenth Century.

Then a new revolution in science was at hand, in the successive breakthroughs of Bernhard Riemann, Albert Einstein, and Max Planck. But the idea of human nature and nature's God that had been at the core of the American Revolution, and which drove those great scientists, was directly attacked by the likes of Bertrand Russell, who held an abiding hatred of mankind, and especially science-driven industrial development. The attack was begun by a school led by the mathematician David Hilbert, which aimed to replace the human mind by logic-ruled axiomatic systems modeled on the failed Euclid.

The combined impact of Hilbert's 1900 presentation to an international mathematics conference seeking to axiomatize all human knowledge, and Russell's direct assault on Einstein and Planck, has undermined the morality of Western Civilization. Lyndon LaRouche has made clear the critical and unique role of these two characters in the horrors of the recent 100 years.

The typical American, especially, would fail to understand how this could be so. How could a mathematician and a so-called philosopher have such an effect?

The fact that this question would arise, indicates the problem. It is the *culture*, the hegemonic ideas about man and nature, that determine the development of the individual and the science produced. The view of human nature expressed by Hilbert and Russell has been the leading factor in both the ending of true science, and the consequent immorality.

The same destructive process in music, at the same tragic historical moment, is discussed in a following article.

Mathematical Rigor (Mortis)

In August of 1900, Hilbert, as a leading mathematician from Göttingen University, was invited to present a future for mathematics, at the international Congress of Mathematics. His proposal involved 23 problems to be solved, although he only read 10 of them in his presentation. It is in this presentation that the program of reducing knowledge to axioms is, in fact, laid out.

While Hilbert identified a number of individual problems, such as Fermat's theorem, the crucial feature is Hilbert's program of proving the formal basis of mathematics through its reduction to logic, and the reduction of physical science to an axiomatic system. In essence, this program of reductionism has fundamentally reigned ever since, regardless of denials.

Russell had spent time in the 1890s in Göttingen, and was encouraged by this program to move to axiomatize Arithmetic in his *Principia Mathematica*, modeled on Newton and Euclid. Keep in mind that by 1900, the latter two had been fundamentally discredited by the work of Riemann regarding Euclid as well as Newton. But, ignoring Riemann, the whole model for

National Archives

The devastation of World War I, being surveyed by an American soldier at Montfaucon, France, 1918.

Hilbert's project was Euclid, stripped of specific axioms and reduced to the form of axiomatizing.

To quote the problems as Hilbert stated them: Number two in his list was "To investigate the consistency of the Arithmetic axioms"; and number six, "To axiomatize those physical sciences in which mathematics plays an important role."

For a science to be valid, it must be of this type, as Hilbert later expressed the primacy of mathematical rigor for physics. And "progress" must be the reduction of science to this form of mathematical rigor.

This meant that all of science in principle, as well as our view of the universe, reduces to a minimum of accepted truths and rules of derivation. Such a system could then be proven only to be *consistent and complete* by a formal proof. It would contain all, and only, the truths of arithmetic, physics, etc. There would be nothing new in the universe. Scholars would merely deduce the truths and wait to find the corresponding experience.

This is much of what we see practiced today, for example in the so-called Standard Model of the universe.

What Hilbert and Russell did was to make deduction the only standard of truth. But with this view, there is no creative human mind that represents access to the real world, and it is the hegemony of this outlook that marks the decline of intellectual morality in the Twentieth Century.

Against Creative Discovery

This attack on creativity occurred just as science had been brought to the verge of a complete revolution, based on the creation of fundamentally new principles upon which to base our understanding and action in the universe in which we exist.

In 1900 Planck discovered the Quantum in which radiation was packaged, contrary to the simple continuum idea of electro-magnetic radiation that had existed until then. This was followed by Einstein's Special, and then later General, Relativity from 1905 to 1912-1915, which changed entirely our concept of Space-Time; and Einstein's hypothesis of the photon—the quantum of light—as well.

Also reflecting the potential for a higher-order breakthrough, was the work of Louis Pasteur, Pierre Curie, and Vladimir Vernadsky. The possibility of developing Physics from the standpoint of life, and more, was at hand.

Of these three, only Vernadsky survived much past 1900, and he was increasingly committed to the question of life in its relation to the non-living; or, better put, that we have to know the non-living from the standpoint of the living. In this regard he saw the work of Curie on dissymmetry as critical. Vernadsky's hypothesis later took the form of whether we could identify the changes in Space-Time that occurred in Life and even in the Mind.

Precisely this constellation of new or hypothesized principles remain the direction in which science needs to go, a century later.

The work of Planck, Einstein, and Vernadsky formed a potential triad, like the one identified by Lyndon LaRouche that led to the achievements of the Renaissance: Brunelleschi, Cusa, and Kepler. As in the first triad, we have the microcosm, the macrocosm, and the systemic unity of the two.

Such a scientific revolution can only be brought to

fruition by the creation of a new system, beyond the reach of, but subsuming, prior ideas. This would mean not giving up causality, but rather a new systemic conception of cause. Einstein, for example, once said, that causality in the quantum realm may be more like a Bach fugue.

On the contrary, *creative change* in human knowledge and capability was ruled out by Hilbert and Russell as a standard of truth or knowability. Russell took this to a dark extreme of pseudo-scientific pessimism and cynicism about humanity, becoming over the ensuing 60 years one of the most famous, and the most evil man of the Twentieth Century.

Morality Destroyed

To get at the destruction wrought by this, one has to grasp the moral dimension. This lies in the nature of LaRouche's physical economy conception, as it developed from the political and economic conception of Alexander Hamilton.

The critical distinction of LaRouche's physical economy is the recognition that value in human economy is the production of a growth in the development of the powers of labor. This is what Hamilton calls artificial labor. It is the production of the capacity for creativity. In reality, value lies in a higher order of activity than we are presently capable of. It is the future potential, systemically, of the power and extension of the reach of that power into new domains of the Universe, which is value. Value is always systemic, and lies in the potential future. It can never be limited to a system, it can never be axiomatic or deductive. This is the nature of man, as economics is the science of the reproduction of the human species. We do not reproduce ourselves as animals do, merely biologically.

This also gives us insight into the Twentieth Century, its wars, its degeneration, and the seminal role of Hilbert and Russell. By their definitions, there was no human mind, no creativity, no action on the future, and therefore no moral purpose, no mission for the human species. Thus there was no reason for the individual to exist.

In fact, all of modern economics, from Adam Smith to game theory, rests itself on this premise of the amorality of the humankind. The effort to effect the future—call it government, society, or as you wish—is to be ruled out as interference in the workings of nature. From there, it is a relatively short step to treat the poor as biological failures, to countenance euthanasia for the sick and elderly, to see a war of all against all in society,

and to promote depopulation—Russell's favorite. For this system of monetarism, value lies not in human beings but in the price of financial instruments, without regard to any change in productivity. It is far from an accident that by the end of the Twentieth Century, nearly all "top" investment bank and hedge fund speculative traders had been educated as mathematicians, and this continued true after the crash they brought on us in 2008.

That Hilbert and Russell led to this is not an accidental feature of their theoretical outlook. Hilbert makes it clear that the real world is subordinate to the rigor of an axiomatic system. To quote a favorable biographer, Constance Reid, "But as a mathematician he was disturbed by a certain lack of order in the triumphs of the physicists." Then, "A few fundamental phenomena should be set up as the axioms from which all observable data could then be derived by rigorous mathematical deduction as smoothly and as satisfyingly as the theorems of Euclid had been derived from his axioms. But this project required a mathematician."[1]

The case of Russell has been covered extensively by Lyndon LaRouche, both in *EIR* and in a major *Fidelio* article in 1994, "How Bertrand Russell Became an Evil Man."[2] Here I will only add some material that gives us an insight into his uniquely oligarchic hatred of humanity in its creative form.

One such example is from a Russell biographer, himself a British philosopher, who began writing the biography as an admirer. In the introduction to his second volume he says:

> The second thought that has come to dominate my reaction to Russell, particularly in the latter half of his life, is how emotionally maimed he was. He was, it sometimes seems, simply not capable of loving another human being,... In many of his political writings this notion appears as the duty to love humanity in the sense of regarding all mankind as, in some sense, coextensive with one's own ego.... He was unable to conceive of loving a person unless he could regard that person as part of himself.[3]

---

1. Reid, Constance. *Hilbert*, Berlin, New York, Springer Verlag, 1970, p. 127.
2. LaRouche, Lyndon. "How Bertrand Russell Became an Evil Man," *Fidelio*, Fall 1994, available at www.schillerinstitute.org.
3. Monk, Ray. *Bertrand Russell, The Ghost of Madness, 1921-1970*, The Free Press, New York, N.Y., 2000, p. 12.

Creative Commons/Ria Novosti

The devastation of World War II: The center of the city of Stalingrad after liberation from the German occupation, February 1943.

And so it was. This is the Russell, who, despite later denials, advocated the "preventive" use of nuclear weapons against the Soviet Union on at least 12 separate occasions between 1945 and 1948. Later he cynically led the anti-nuclear counterculture of the 1950s and '60s.

Perhaps the best example of the pure evil of Russell is a short story he wrote in his 30s or 40s entitled "Satan in the Suburbs." In it, he effectively writes through his fantasy of wiping out humanity, as a consequence of his doing battle with a satanic figure who ultimately convinces him of the irretrievable horror of human beings. Russell as a figure builds a doomsday device, expressing his hatred of people and science.

Giving Up On Reality

The culmination of the mathematical suppression of science occurred as a direct attack on its opposite, the man LaRouche has called the only competent scientist in the United States in the Twentieth Century, Albert Einstein.

At the International Solvay Conference of 1927 and then again in 1930, all the leading figures had direct or indirect ties to Hilbert and Göttingen, such as Born, Heisenberg, Bohr, and others. Their line against Einstein was simply this: In light of the problems arising in Quantum Mechanics, we should give up knowing what occurs in reality; we should accept the mathematical model as all one can say. This is, in fact, the hallmark of positivism. Those like Einstein who insisted on a real physics, were dinosaurs, stuck in a Classical picture of causality. Mathematics, said the Solvay Conferences, is the only truth. We remain only to deduce.

Einstein argued effectively against this, and continued to do so despite the attempt to ridicule him, which continues to this day. But the media and academic verdict went to the mathematicians, the agnostics, or perhaps in some cases, the atheists. Einstein's deity had given us the ability to know the creation.

What we are left with is a new version of Ptolemy and his epicycles, only today applied to particles. Left open is what is the reality. For those who adhered to the positivist dogma like Heisenberg, the theory was complete. Einstein, as Plato before and Kurt Gödel after him, knew there was no such system.

This was the end of a process begun with the attack on Riemann for his "lack of rigor," by Weierstrass, Klein, and Hilbert. Perhaps the leading case of this was Riemann's use of the Dirichlet's Principle, which was derided by Weierstrass. This is a principle of minimization that indeed works in physics, but lacks a complete formal proof.

Given the role of Riemann and Gauss before him, as scientists developing a new mathematical language subordinated to the needs of science, what began with the attacks on Riemann was a direct negation of the creative scientific discoveries that had driven the Nineteenth Century.

Today we are left with a reduction of creative mind to neural networks, of justice to giving chimpanzees—nasty creatures on their own—the legal standing of persons, and a recurrence of artificial intelligence fantasies, even though this has been known to be fallacious since Plato's *Parmenides*.

Unless we recognize that it is creativity alone that defines us and, that it is also itself the standard of truth, we will fail in the mission given to us by the Nature of the Universe. This is what the Twentieth Century crime of David Hilbert and Bertrand Russell has taken from us.

The Murder of Music With the Death of Brahms

by Mindy Pechenuk

"Mankind is a unique species! There is nothing like it, there's no animal that's like it. There's no animal which produces mankind. Mankind is a unique phenomenon. And the characteristic of mankind is creativity! And therefore, what you want to do in life, you want to accompany your life with things like great music. Because they perpetuate your existence by perpetuating what you're capable of doing for mankind.

"That's why you want to do a good performance, because immortality is looking at you—and raising questions. Here we're talking now about music, but the point is that's what the reason of music is. The meaning is not based on music; it's based on the soul of mankind."

—*Lyndon LaRouche,*
May 10, 2015

Johannes Brahms. With his death in 1897, creative beauty, as the lodestar of centuries of musical composition, went dark. The music of bestial "emotions," that of Brahms' opposites Liszt and Wagner, was heavily funded and promoted to become "modern music."

The Twentieth Century was a century of cultural, scientific, political destruction, and this was as deliberate as the assassination of Abraham Lincoln, William McKinley, John F. Kennedy, and Robert Kennedy. It was as deliberate as the election of the Bush family, and Barack Obama. It was as deliberate as World War I and II, Korea, Vietnam, the Iraq war, and today the threat of thermonuclear war. This was the conscious aim of the British Empire, their Wall Street allies, and others, as they drove to carry out their hideous policy of killing off the human species. The most deadly tool they had was to eradicate the knowability of the human mind as the driving force in the universe.

Therefore, the purpose of this discussion, is to locate for you, the reader, the fight that took place in the sacred domain of Classical music before you were born, or in some cases during your lifetime. It is not too late to destroy this evil, to find the beauty in the true creative human mind, and the real love, passion, and mission that we all share for the benefit of future generations to come. Unto the stage of history we now travel—only to come out of this with a new, and heightened understanding, so that we are to succeed in creating a new alliance of nations through real classical beauty and science—it is possible and necessary!

Turn of a Dark Age

Let us step back from the Twentieth Century, into the latter half of the Nineteenth Century where the battle between Zeus and Prometheus was still an upfront fight. The last Classical musical Promethean was Johannes Brahms, and all that was needed by the British Empire (et al.) was Brahms' death in 1897 to unleash horrors upon humanity. However, the stage was set before Brahms' death. For us today, like Brahms, the mission to create new relations among nations, to bring about a human creative world, is a continuous battle for the soul and mind of mankind. This was the same passionate mission which inspired Beethoven, Mendelssohn, Schubert, the Schumanns, and Brahms, to transform mankind from the grip of one of the most evil Zeusians of music, Franz Liszt, and his ally Richard Wagner.

By the end of the Nineteenth Century, the British Empire was desperate to stop what was progressing against their control of the world; they needed a new war, and a dark age. The Empire acted, and the world dramatically changed—the 1890 ouster of Bismark as chancellor of Germany-the necessary step to set the stage for World War I; and the 1890 assassination of the President of France Sadi Carnot, which unleashed both a political and musical hell from the worst quarters of France, and in Vienna under the influence of the British Empire crowd. Only to follow with the Dreyfus Affair, which was crucial, not only for the political destruction of Europe and the world, but also the cultural destruction. All of this was done to stop what Hamilton, Abraham Lincoln, McKinley, and others had set into motion throughout the world.

Johannes Brahms, the last of the musical geniuses alive, set the standard for all humanity—all of his other friends were dead, and he carried with him the responsibility, passion, love for future generations, to know (not to just understand) what is it that makes us human. Once he had died, the standard-bearer was no longer there, and within three years of his death—hell was let loose with the Twentieth Century. But, much to the dismay of the British Empire and Wall Street, there were individuals, who rose to the occasion from the destruction of the Twentieth Century—Lyndon LaRouche, Wilhelm Furtwängler, Norbert Brainin, Albert Einstein, Vladimir Vernadsky, and Max Planck.

Now, we are in the final months of that fight!

Friedrick Liszt (1811-1886), with Richard Wagner, were the leading musical adversaries of Brahms and Giuseppe Verdi—and of creative reason in music—during the second half of the 19th Century.

Brahms' Mind, Liszt's Fingers

Brahms was both a true patriot of his country, Germany,[1] and a universal citizen of the world. He was a close friend of Chancellor Bismarck, It was known that Brahms' library contained Bismarck's letters and speeches, some of which he carried with him on trips. He openly spoke of Bismarck, and the need for German unity, which he would celebrate in his musical compositions.

There is a famous moment when his young student Gustav Jenner enlisted in his regiment, and Brahms is on record saying to Jenner: "I cannot say how I envy you. If I were only as young as you are I should go with you at once, but that too I missed."[2]

Brahms' library was rich with every aspect of Classical life from Schiller, Lessing, Goethe, Aeschylus, Homer, Sophocles. "His contact with pioneers of medical science kept him abreast of the latest developments. His close friendships with Billroth and Engelmann account for his owning a copy of Billroth's *Surgical Letters* and Engelmann's *Experiments on the Microscopic Changes in Muscle Contraction*: indeed, he would observe, along with the students, Billroth's pioneering surgery at the University Hospital in Vienna. The worlds of scientific invention earned his attention as well, and he was interested in the introduction of electricity in Vienna and the development of the Edison system."[3]

Without Franz Liszt, and his ally Richard Wagner, the destruction of the Twentieth Century would not have been possible. The long fingers of Liszt reached across the centuries, into both the United States and Europe. It was the spinoffs of Liszt that helped to shape the Twentieth Century destruction, with the aid of others yet to come. The eulogy that Liszt wrote upon

---

1. Contrary to popular opinion today, music, science, art, drama, and nation-building are a unity.

2. Musgrave, Michael. *A Brahms Reader*, Sheridan Books, Michigan, 200, p. 175.

3. *Ibid.*, pp. 172-173.

Bridgeman Art Library

"Franz Lizst Fantasizing at the Piano," by Josef Danhauser. The German Classical poet Heinrich Heine nailed the Wagnerian Romantics in a satirical poem, as rutting cats "conceiving of" their latest compositions on a shrieking rooftop: "Ohh, Liszt! You glorious tomcat!" howls the lucky female.

the death of his loyal ally Napoleon III speaks for itself:

"Magnanimous heart, all encompassing mind, practical, gentle, and generous character—and sinister fate! A hamstrung and garroted Caesar—but moved by a breath of the divine Caesar, ideal personification of the earthly empire!... I believed sincerely ... that Napoleon's government was the most suited to the needs and progress of our times. He gave great examples, and accomplished or attempted great deeds.... However terrible it was, his final disaster does not erase them! When justice comes—France will bring back his coffin to place it in glory next to that of Napoleon I, in the Church of the Invalides!... the Emperor filled his life with the constant exercise of those most synonymous sovereign virtues: charity, goodness, liberality, generosity, magnificence, munificence.... his gratitude to those who had done him some favor.... I try to imitate him himself, blessing his memory and praying for him to the God of mercies who has made nations capable of healing."[4]

This eulogy was no spur-of-the-moment action. Franz Liszt was close to Napoleon and his circles for many years. Liszt would not only visit Napoleon, but

Liszt's son-in-law, Émile Ollivier, was an aide to Napoleon whom Liszt would confer with for political objectives. Let there be no misunderstanding—Franz "Zeus" Liszt was a political operative of the British Empire—and his music speaks to this directly.[5] Liszt and his side-agent of influence Richard Wagner, deployed every moment to destroy the true spirit and passion of the creative nature of man.

The battle of the late Nineteenth Century was clear to Brahms, and the circle of his collaborators, and for them, the epistemological and political battle was one. As Liszt and Wagner through their music created a degenerate, pessimistic mankind—pissing on all the great minds that came before; i.e., J.S. Bach, Mozart, Beethoven, Schiller, Leibniz, Kepler—Brahms and the Schumanns created the optimistic creative mankind, with the passion and love for the future. According to Brahms' good friend George Henschel:[6]

... "a volume of the 'Forty-Eight' was invariably open on the piano of his apartment. When Henschel noticed it, Brahms commented, 'With this I rinse my mouth every morning.' And when Brahms sat down to play to others, it was invariably the 'Forty-Eight'[7] that came to mind. ..."

Brahms, like those in his circle of friends, and Beethoven and Mozart before, returned to the master J.S. Bach. Brahms et al. were driven by the science of the human mind—by the creative spirit of lawful "universal principles," by the creation of truth as expressed in metaphor. In this case, let Brahm's student Florence May speak to this:

"His interpretation of Bach was always unconventional and quite unfettered by traditional theory, and he certainly did not share the opinion, which has had many

---

4. Letter 148 from Liszt to Agnes Klindworth.

5. Compare <u>Mozart's "Ave Verum" with Liszt's "Ave Verum"</u> Think about what the difference implies about the nature of Prometheus versus Zeus. There is much to say on this matter, but for our purposes here I will leave that for another discussion.

6. Henschel was both a well-known baritone and a conductor who would later conduct the Boston Symphony.

7. J.S. Bach's *Well-Tempered Clavier*.

distinguished adherents, that Bach's music should be performed in a simply flowing style. In the movements of the Suites he liked variety of tone and touch, as well as a certain elasticity of 'tempo'. His playing of many of the preludes and some of the fugues was a revelation of exquisite poems, and he performed them not only with graduated shadings but with marked contrasts of tone, effect. Each note of Bach's passages and figures contributed, in the hands of Brahms, to form melody which was instinct with feeling of some kind or other. It might be deep pathos or light-hearted playfulness and jollity; impulsive energy or soft and tender grace' but sentiment (as distinct from sentimentality) was always there: monotony never. 'Quite tender and quite soft' was his frequent admonition to me, whilst in another place he required the utmost impetuosity.

"Brahms particularly loved Bach's suspensions. 'It is here that it must sound,' he would say, pointing to the tied note and insisting, whilst not allowing me to force the preparation, that the latter should be so struck as to give the fullest possible effect to the dissonance. 'How am I to make this sound?' I asked him of a few bars of a subject lying for the third, fourth and fifth fingers of the left hand, which he wished brought out clearly, but in a very soft tone. 'You must think particularly of the fingers with which you play it, and by and by it will come out,' he answered."[8]

On the other hand, Franz Liszt showed his clearly his hatred for mankind, and was notorious for pounding so hard on the piano, that he was constantly breaking strings, and would often need a second piano during his performances!

The assassination of President Sadi Carnot of France, contrary to popular myth, was not just carried out by a bunch of anarchists. This was deployed by the British Empire, as was the Dreyfus Affair, as was the dismissal of Chancellor Bismarck of Germany. France now became the center for musical pessimism; anything created by J.S. Bach, Mozart, Haydn, Beethoven, Schubert, Schumann, and Brahms was written out of history. Springing up everywhere in Paris was the insanity of Berlioz, Satie, Ravel, Fauré, Saint-Saëns, Debussy, D'Indy, Princess Polignac (nee Winnaretta Singer of the Singer Sewing Machine Family). Why do I say insanity? Because their music has left the domain of human creativity. They are the successors of the insanity of Franz Liszt and this Zeusian school.

Franz Liszt created a cult around him whether at his shrine in Weimar, in Paris, or wherever he went. His sidekick Wagner, and the Bayreuth orgies of his operas, provided a central place for this network of early fascists to reside. By 1888-1896 Debussy, Bernard Shaw to Maurice Barres would come together at Bayreuth. The working relationship between Debussy and Barres continued in the 1900s.

Ask yourself, what happens when you destroy truth and universal principles? Since J.S. Bach's creation of the Well-Tempered Bel Canto art of musical composition, the standard was set for music. J.S. Bach lived in the domain of Plato, Cusa, Kepler, and Leibniz. Bach created through his compositions a living "future of the future."

Ideas for Bach, like those who developed these universal principles—i.e., Mozart, Haydn, Beethoven, Schubert, Clara and Robert Schumann, and Brahms—were not contained in the notes, or fixed intervals or harmonic relations. The principle of metaphor was their domain—in which you could only know truth through the paradoxes they created, in their mind and soul, to yours. If you try to literally play or sing the notes on the page, you will have become the "practical man" that the Empire wants you to be—a good slave to kill yourself, and all of humanity. For Bach et al., they were continuing to create new universal harmonies, from the one in their mind. The future was their guide, taking your mind and soul to higher resolutions throughout their

On Musical Tuning

From Bach through Mozart, Haydn, Beethoven, Shubert, Schumann, Brahms, and Verdi the tuning of music was at C=256. This was not arbitrary. It is not a metrical figure, but rather is a physical space-time development of the human mind. It is tied to the question of poetry, metaphor, the harmonics of the universe. What was done by the British Empire and Wall Street to both raise the official tuning to A=440—which was done by Goebbels, Hitler's propaganda minister—and to destroy composition through Stravinsky, Debussy, Schoenberg, has led to the creation of the practical and irrational man, a world without a knowable truth.

—*Mindy Pechenuk*

8. *Brahms Reader*, pp. 127-128.

Library of Congress

Modern music's "goddess," Nadia Boulanger, with composer Aaron Copland (left) and money man Walter Piston in 1945.

Symphony Society (1878), and also conducted at the Metropolitan Opera. Leopold's son Walter made his conducting debut at the Metropolitan Opera (1885) conducting Wagner's "Tannhauser." After his father's death, Walter took over both the Oratorio Society and the New York Symphony, and formed the Damrosch Opera Company(1894), from whose platforms he played a critical role in destroying the minds of mankind.

The extraordinary role carried out by the "godsons" of Franz Liszt—Walter Damrosch, and his brother Frank—was crucial in shaping the destruction of the Twentieth Century. While Walter Damrosch was instrumental in the trans-Atlantic operations, Frank Damrosch helped dominate the minds of the young generations of upcoming artists, and I would add, the population as a whole, in the United States. He was responsible for helping to establish the "Institute of Musical Art" in New York, which was later became known as "Juillard School of Music," while his sister Clara Damrosch, and her husband David Mannes established the "Mannes College, The New School of Music" in 1916 in Manhattan. The education of American culture was clearly dominated to destroy the United States. World War I not only took the physical life of many throughout the world, but, it also took the cultural mind and soul and replaced it with the "practical" man!

compositions. This was not true for Franz Liszt, Richard Wagner, Berlioz, Strauss, Satie, Ravel, <u>Debussy</u>, Fauré, Saint-Saëns, and those who came after them. For them there is no future, no longer an understanding of the immortality of our mankind—reaching to create breakthroughs to develop a higher power of mankind in the universe—no universal principles, no hypothesis. All they are left with is a smelly pessimism and a feeling of failure—and what we have in today's culture is the bottom of this pit.

Vienna was no different. In fact, Vienna was Brahms' last battleground, where he lived out the remaining years of his life, and was in direct battle with Wagner (died 1883), Liszt (died 1886), Mahler, Bruckner, Freud, and Boltzmann.

Battling for America

The British Empire had its long-term mission in mind to destroy all of humanity, and between the 1890s and the early Twentieth Century, they had declared musical/cultural warfare on the United States. One route into the United States was through New York, the secondary route was through Boston.

Both Liszt and Brahms deployed their forces to the New World (the United States). It was Leopold Damrosch (1832-85), a longtime friend of Liszt and Wagner, who arrived with his family in New York City (1871) and founded the Oratorio Society in 1873, the New York

Comes the Congress of Cultural Freedom

Now we arrive at the pit of the Twentieth Century: 1900-1927 (from the International Congress of Mathematicians in 1900 to the Solvay Conference in 1927). The British Empire and Wall Street forces declared war on the human mind/soul and nation state. Hilbert and Bertrand Russell created the practical mathematical mind at the International Congress of Mathematicians. (see article in this issue). The same operation was being carried out in music. The flood gates were open, and what entered became total reductionism, anarchy in the music world. In April of 1900, Paris is the home of the Universal Exposition, where there was an exhibition to carry out the same destruction in music: as in the case of Ernest Boulanger (the father of Nadia Boulanger, whom you will come to know soon) who "had been invited to have the score of one of his choral works displayed … in an exhibit devoted to French contemporary musicians at the Universal Exposition of 1900."[9]

Now the deed was done, and the monster had been unleashed. Brahms had only been dead three years and the musical scene was already dominated by the likes of the Damrosch Family, the Boulanger Family, Stravinsky, Diaghilev, Debussy, Fauré, Ravel, Princess Polignac, Cocteau, Schoenberg.[10]

By 1910 (only 13 years after Brahms' death) Stravinsky had scribbled on paper "The Firebird" (1910), "Petrushka" (1911) and "Le Sacre du Printemps"—"The Rite of Spring" (1913). What an assault against humanity is Stravinsky's "Rite of Spring"—a ballet based on a ritual human sacrifice. What does that say about the immortality special to humankind. Compare that to

---

9. Rosenstiel, Léonie. *Nadia Boulanger, A Life in Music*, W.W. Norton & Co., New York, 1982, p. 40.

10. The current popular argument that Schoenberg was different than Stravinsky, is like arguing that Hitler and Mussolini were different. Schoenberg's "12 tone row system," which is pure mathematical reductionism, is in the end no different than the neurotic pounding of anarchist rhythms, and screeching noises of Stravinksy.

Brahm's composing his "Vier Ernste Gesange" "Four Serious Songs" After the stroke of his dear friend Clara Schumann. Brahms through the four songs developed the beauty and truth on what it is to be human—ending with the fourth song based on Saint Paul's 1 Corinthians 13, "If I have not *agape*, I am nothing."

How far away is Stravinsky from the video games, and violence which today's culture calls "entertainment?"

The defenders of Stravinsky were a clique which included Debussy-who became very close to Stravinsky. Debussy wrote to Stravinsky in November 1913 from Paris: "Our reading at the piano of *Le Sacre du Printemps* is always in my mind. It haunts me like a beautiful dream, and I try in vain to reinvoke the terrific impression. That is why I wait for the stage performance like a greedy child impatient for promised sweets."[11]

Let us be clear—Debussy is not a "child"; his musical intention is completely destructive, and at its roots destroys the universal principle that J.S. Bach had created with the Well-Tempered Bel Canto compositions.

---

11. Stravinsky, Vera. *Stravinsky In Pictures and Documents*, Simon & Schuster, N.Y., 1978, p. 90.

Schizophrenia or Sanity

"One no longer feels dominated by the phrase, the literal meaning of the words. Cast in an immutable mold which adequately expresses their value, they do not require any further commentary. The text thus becomes purely phonetic material for the composer. He can dissect it at will and concentrate all his attention on its primary constituent element—that is to say, on the syllable."

—*Stravinsky, from his autobiography*

"Furtwängler's performance is a very clinically crucial thing. Everything about that is total suspension. And the suspension is totally controlled. When you hear, experience, the Furtwängler version (Schubert 9th Symphony, Furtwängler/Berlin Philharmonic Orchestra) and you hear it in reasonable concern, you do not hear it in sections.

"You have a kind of religious experience, which starts out, in a sense, instructing you morally, at an opening. And then it goes through—like the second movement—it goes in a certain way which is almost magical. And most people, as conductors, couldn't do it. They butcher it, with rhythmic routines. They don't see where the progress is, in the process of movement. They don't see the daring explosion, which is effected by Furtwangler's direction, at that point. And then the finale, the effect of that—Boom! Boom! This is charged! This is Schubert!…

"Take the case of the Schubert Ninth Symphony. That performance under his direction is a unified piece which contains no separations in the process of delivering the composition. And anyone who does divide it into parts is making an ass of themselves. Because the idea is that you are captured by a transition from one phase to another phase. It's a phase-relationship. It's not a composition of parts of the composition; it's a process of a progressive process. And Schubert, of course, did that!"

—*Lyndon LaRouche, May 10, 2015*

For the great geniuses of the Eighteenth and Nineteenth Centuries, the subject of every scientific discovery or musical composition, was the universal nature of man. For Debussy, Nadia Boulanger, and the musicians in France around the "Action-Française," there was a different view of man. For this I will let Debussy himself speak from March of 1915: "For many years now I have been saying the same thing: that we have been unfaithful to the musical traditions of our race for more than a century and a half.... Since Rameau, we have no purely French tradition.... Today when the virtues of our race are being exalted, the victory should give our artists a sense of purity and remind them of the nobility of French blood."

And again, Debussy in a letter to Stravinsky in October 1915: "It will be necessary to cleanse the world of this bad seed. It will be necessary to kill the microbe of false grandeur, or organized ugliness, which we have not perceived as simply beings of weakness.... You are assuredly one of those who could victoriously combat the other gasses that are just as lethal as the other, and against which we had not masks."[12]

This tradition of fascist identity was ramped at the time. In the case of Nadia Boulanger, the "goddess" of music, she was known for her beliefs that "Jews were members of another race, however, and she tried to avoid having 'too many' in her classes at any one time."[13]

With that introduction to Nadia Boulanger, a few words must be said. She is someone who is known very well in the institutions of music, but not to the general public. Almost every musician, young and old, traveled to study, to sit at her feet, and worship at her altar. I was introduced to Nadia, when I was in undergraduate school at Queens College in NYC. Unfortunately my music theory professor, Leo Kraft, was one of her students, and he, like many others, continued the disaster called American Music which started after World War I.

The British Empire and Wall Street didn't wait for the end of World War I to escalate their cultural warfare—on April 6, 1917, in the midst of World War I, Walter Damrosch became the first president of the newly founded American Friends of Musicians in France. With the aid of the British Empire and Wall Street, the end to nation-states and scientific progress was unfolding.

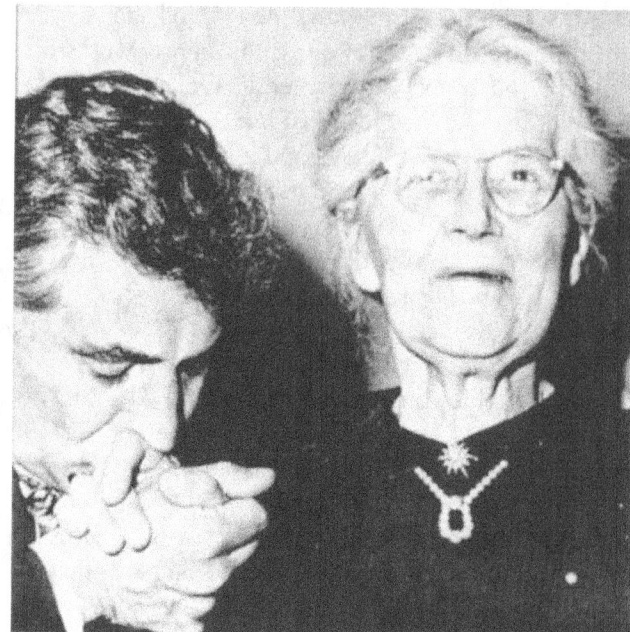

"Pop" music crossover Leonard Bernstein kisses Boulanger's hand after she conducted the New York Philharmonic in a February 1962 concert.

Today, while we are in such a critical period in Germany where the trio of Foreign Minister Steinmeier and former Chancellors Schmidt and Schroeder can reverse what the current Chancellor Merkel is doing, and re-establish Germany's relationship to working with Russia, therefore avoiding thermonuclear war, most people do not see this, because of the destruction of Classical thinking at the turn of the Twentieth Century. But, Lyndon LaRouche does not only see it, but acts on the solution. Why? Because Lyndon LaRouche is a Promethean!

This project to destroy the minds of both America and Europe coming out of World War I was, as today, financed with the blood money of Wall Street and the British Empire. Some of the key financiers and activist were Harry Harkness Flagler (his family is the fascist Standard Oil Company), John D. Rockefeller, the Vanderbilts, Henry C. Frick, Mrs. William Astor Chanler, and Mrs. George Montgomery Tuttle.[14]

The conditions to carry out cultural warfare were now in place, and with the Armistice signed, and World War I over, the beginning of World War II was put in place. It was Walter Damrosch and General Pershing that immediately organized the "French High Command" to set up a school for the training of

---

12. Both letters quoted from Jane F. Fulcher, *The Composer As Intellectual, Music and Ideology in France, 1914-1940.*
13. Rosenstiel, *op. cit.*, p. 198.

14. Rosenstiel, *op. cit.*, p. 136.

"American bandmasters" and by the "summer of 1919, it was in full operation in Chaumont, under the direction of Francis Casadesus." The next step was taken by Damrosch and Nadia Boulanger, to set up a permanent school for teaching Americans music—this became known as Fountainbleau (the American Conservatory in Fountainbleau, France).

The school had its first official class in 1921. It is at that moment in 1921 that Nadia began Wednesday Salon meetings at her house. Here the students gathered at her altar and were brainwashed in the "anal" practical, formal analysis of Bach, Mozart, Beethoven, Schumann, Schubert, and Brahms. By the end of sessions you were convinced there are no Universal Principles, only particulars, chords, structures—the human mind was destroyed. At the same time Nadia would encourage all the "new music of the Twentieth Century"—Stravinsky, Valery, Fauré were some among the establishment in Paris who would attend the Wednesday sessions.

Creative Commons

The American Conservatory in Fontainebleau, France, started in 1921 by Boulanger and the Damrosch family, blunted the enduring force of Beethoven's, Mozart's, and Bach's music by "analyzing" it into chords, tone structures, etc. Generations of composers were taught to use these "structures" like pieces in a jigsaw puzzle.

Nadia's "American Students," starting with Aaron Copland in 1921, were the predominant voices heard in the United States along with Virgil Thompson, Elliot Carter, Roy Harris, Walter Piston (whose text book on harmony is used to brainwash many generations of music students), and Roger Sessions, just to name a few. Late in his life, Lenard Bernstein went to meet "the goddess" Nadia for her approval! It is no accident that Nadia Boulanger, like her other associates at "Action-Français," share the same view of mankind as Debussy, Barres, Liszt, Wagner, and Monteverdi.[15]

Boulanger vs. Furtwängler in America

Finally in 1924, plans emerged to bring Nadia to the United States. Once again she was sponsored by Walter Damrosch, and his New York Symphony Society, of which none other than Harry Harkness Flagler was the president. Nadia's concert tour started with a first performance in New York with Damrosch conducting the New York Symphony, and, then went to Boston, for a performance with the Boston Symphony under the baton of Koussevitzky.

For Nadia's first entrance formally into America, neither Beethoven nor Brahms is played; instead Nadia deploys her former student Aaron Copland to write a special composition for her for Organ and Orchestra. Copland joined the faculty of the New School in New York in about 1927.

At the time Nadia was to give her opening concert in New York, on January 11, 1925 featuring the premier of Copeland's "Symphony for Organ and Orchestra," she was met with a great surprise. The great genius Wilhelm Furtwängler arrived for the first time in New York, and was to give his first concert in New York with the New York Philharmonic. It was only days after Furtwängler conducted the New York Philharmonic that Stravinsky was there to conduct an all-Stravinsky concert with the Philharmonic. So, here we find the battle ground from Liszt through to the Damrosch family, and others, inviting all the degenerates to conduct, or perform with the New York Symphony

---

15. Nadia was part of a project to revive Monteverdi, who was the leader of the art of reductionism in the late 1500s into the 1600s against Plato, Socrates, da Vinci, Cusa, and Kepler.

Society, and the New York Philharmonic: From Nadia Boulanger, Maurice Ravel, Toscanini, George Gershwin, and many more.

By 1928, one year after the 1927 Solvay Conference where Einstein was attacked, the New York Symphony and the New York Philharmonic merged into The Philharmonic Symphony Orchestra of New York, Inc.; Clarence MacKay, Chairman and Harry Harkness Flagler, President. At the end of 1928 Gershwin (one of Nadia's students at Foutainbleau) gave the world premier of his "American in Paris," with Walter Damrosch conducting.

Let the 'Trumpets Sound'

In the midst of the insanity of the Twentieth Century, the voice of "immortality" was heard as Furtwängler did two more tours of the United States, ending his last performance with Brahms' Requiem. Furtwängler and Brahms "sounded the trumpet" to Americans to wake up and leave the bestial world behind, and find their souls in the beauty of development—in the principles of Hamilton and the preamble of our Constitution. This was the last tour of America by Furtwängler, who was never allowed in the the United States again.

The British Empire and Wall Street went after Furtwängler, and branded him a Nazi, because he stayed in his country during World War II, and conducted the concerts he hoped would help his fellow man. Furtwängler had to go through the hideous process of de-Nazification. Instead, the real card-carrying Nazi conductor Herbert Von Karajan was given free rein everywhere. His performances of Beethoven, Brahms and all their friends, makes these great minds unknowable to anyone who listens. Along with Von Karajan came Bruno Walter, Arturo Toscanini, and then the pervert Leonard Bernstein taking the reins of the New York Philharmonic.

A similar fight took place in Boston at the same time. As noted earlier, Brahms' friend George Herschel

Igor Stravinsky with Boulanger in 1937. His setting of a barbaric human sacrifice to "music" ("Rite of Spring") was accepted as dynamic emotion by dumbed-down millions in the Twentieth Century.

goes to the Boston Symphony in 1888, followed by the great Arthur Nikisch (1893-1895) who played a big role in Furtwängler's development. After that the Boston Symphony, like New York, falls into the hands of the degenerates such as Serge Alexandrovich Koussevitzky (1924-1949).

The stage was now set for the British Empire, Wall Street, and others to unleash the next phase of their cultural attack: the "Congress for Cultural Freedom" and Hollywood—the place where Stravinsky, Nabokov, Schoenberg, the Huxleys and their satanic crew wound up in America. I will leave that discussion for another time.

There is one more turning point in Twentieth Century history that must not be overlooked—the 1989 fall of the Berlin Wall. Lyndon LaRouche was the only person to forecast this happening in his Kempinski Hotel press conference in 1988. I find once again that irony is the purveyor of "truth." It was in 1989 that Leonard Bernstein went to London to perform his "Candide," which is taken from Voltaire's "Candide," an attack on the Gottfried Leibniz from whom the preamble of our U.S. Constitution comes -"Life, Liberty, and the Pursuit of Happiness." Leibniz played a crucial role in the lives of Benjamin Franklin, Lyndon LaRouche, Einstein, and those of us who have come to discover him today. I will let Bernstein speak for himself, as he addressed his audience in the concert hall of London, in 1989 :

"His (Voltaire's) masterpiece was a tough, skinny little novella called *Candide*, which inspired the playwright Lillian Hellman and me to have a bash at it musically. Voltaire's book was actually entitled *Candide, or Optimism*, it being a viciously satirical attack on a prevalent philosophical system known as Optimism, which was based on the rather indigestible writing of a certain Gottfried Wilhelm von Leibniz and popularized by our own, beloved Alexander Pope, for example in this great line form his "Essay on Man": 'One truth is clear-whatever is, is right.'

"Now, according to Leibniz, whose ideas Pope was lyricizing, if we believe in a Creator, then he must be a good Creator, and the greatest of all possible creators, and therefore could have created only The Best of All Possible Worlds. In other words: 'Everything that is, is right.' Granted that in this world the innocent are mindlessly slaughtered and that crime goes mostly unpunished, that there is disease and death and poverty. But if we could only see the whole picture, the divine and universal plan, then we would understand that whatever happens is for the best. Thus spake Leibniz. Naturally Voltaire found this idea absurd every day of his life, but particularly on that day in 17 55 when all of Lisbon, Portugal exploded in an earthquake, and uncountable numbers of people were drowned, crushed, burned alive, exterminated. Now if Leibniz was right, as said Voltaire, then God is just playfully spraying his flit gun and down go a million mosquitoes, at random, haphazardly…"

To answer this I will let our dear friend Wolfgang Amadeus Mozart speak, as he did in a letter to his father on July 3, 1778 from Paris: "Now I have a piece of news for you which you may have heard already, namely, that that godless arch-rascal Voltaire has pegged out like a dog, like a beast! That is his reward! "

More Chapters To Be Written

To you the reader: While there is much more to say on the matter, what I have presented to you is one chapter of what happened in the Twentieth Century to Classical music. For now, take your lessons from the battle that was waged before most of you were born; or, for those who were born in the Twentieth Century, I hope this gives you a handle on what happened to your mind, soul, nation, world and the universe. The potential of the works and lives of Plato, Cusa, Kepler, Leibniz, Riemann, Einstein, Vernadsky, Planck, J.S. Bach, Mozart, Haydn, Beethoven, Schubert, Schumann, Brahms, and those who did break through in the Twentieth Century like Furtwängler, Norbert Brainin, Lyndon LaRouche (of whom the great first violinist of the Amadeus String Quartet said, "Lyndon LaRouche is the greatest musician alive today") would have us already directing the development of mankind with new generations of symphonies, and string quartets.

Do not let this moment pass: Think, and act in the spirit of truth for the "future of the future" and let us bring about today the greatest victory mankind has ever achieved—and bring our United States, with Germany leading the way in Europe, into the New Just World which is now awaiting us with the development of the BRICS (another mission created by Lyndon and Helga LaRouche, and our movement).

Music Is Immortal

"I live neither in the past nor in the future. I am in the present. I cannot know what tomorrow will bring forth. I can know only what the truth is for me today. That is what I am called upon to serve, and I serve it in lucidity."

—*Stravinsky from his Autobiography*

"The beauty is creativity, *per se*. It's also the measure of what creativity is. So you take any composition— it's a sacred business. If you really want to do it, you're attempting a sacred work. And it's a sense of man's immortality. Even people, when they die, if they live well, they can contribute a memory of beauty, and that's rarely done these days.

"Now we're in one of the greatest periods, the most emotional part of human history that ever existed. We exist on the brink of the threat of the immediate destruction of the human species by the forces that dominate mankind today. Where do you find the passion that will inform you to take the actions which will save mankind from the destruction which is being brought by mankind on himself, on society? That's music. That's art. It's the sense of immortality, that those people who have died did not die in vain. But what they had decided to do is to commit themselves to the future of mankind.

"The beauty of mankind's existence always lies beyond mankind himself. We are able to become the instruments of unleashing the beauty of mankind. Every great composer and every musical performer works on that basis. If they don't do it, they're crap-artists. And I've known a lot of crap-artists."

—*Lyndon LaRouche May 10, 2015 dialogue with associates after an informal evening of music.*

T.H. Huxley's Hideous Revolution In Science

by Paul Glumaz

Introduction

June 4—A hideous revolution took place in the sciences and in our culture during the latter part of the Nineteenth Century, which had the aim of remaking the self-conception of the human species from that of a cognitive and creative being made in the image of the Creator, to that of an instinct-driven ape-like creature. This hideous cultural and scientific revolution has been so successful, that while we live in a world of potentially unlimited scientific progress, our descent into a totally bestial view of man has created both an inability to realize this potential, and with it an existential crisis for the human race.

This hideous revolution was instigated and carried out by a core group of individuals who took over the world's scientific establishments, first in Great Britain, and then later the rest of the world.

The principal organizer, minister of propaganda, and subsequent "pope" of this group was Thomas H. Huxley (1825-1895).

The group based this revolution on the work of Charles Darwin (1809-1882), and used his idea of "natural selection," to create a "religious"-like belief-system to explain "evolution," based on competition, or the "struggle for survival" of the fittest. This belief-system was then extended to all areas of culture, science, and religion.

We call this revolution "Malthusian," because Charles Darwin credited Thomas Malthus as the source of his concept of "natural selection."

Thomas Malthus (1766-1834) was a British East India Company economist, and a professor at Hailey-bury College, the British East India Company's school in London. Malthus's *Essay on Population* popularized the ideas of an earlier Venetian economist, Gianmaria Ortes.

Malthus and Ortes asserted that population always increases at a greater rate than the material means to sustain that population. Darwin, in turn, used this tenet to claim that this population pressure, of more individuals being born than can survive within any species of plant or animal, is the driver which causes nature to select out the "fittest." This process of selection of the "fittest," is the reason that some traits survive in a species, while others do not. This idea of the "fittest" governs the outcome of the variability within a given species, and the creation of new species, or "evolution."

Thomas H. Huxley, depicted in an etching by Leopold Flameng, 1885.

These "fittest" concepts that were developed in biology by Charles Darwin to explain "natural selection," were then extended to the general scientific, social, economic, and cultural realms by Thomas Huxley and his group. An associate of Darwin and Huxley, Herbert Spencer (1820-1903), applied Darwinian "survival of the fittest" in the social and economic realms. It was Spencer who developed the concept of "Social Darwinism." In the economic realm, the Darwinian view was used to justify "free trade" ideology, and the brutal exploitation of subject populations. This included justifying the deliberately-induced famines imposed on colonies such as India and Ireland.

Later these Darwinian notions become the basis of the eugenics movement, that culminated with Adolf Hitler's racial-hygiene approach to the slave labor exploitation and mass murder of undesirables and captive populations.

Eliminate Plato and the 'Augustans'

At the beginning of the Nineteenth Century, with the success of the American Revolution and its implications, there was a profound optimism about what humanity could discover and develop. On the continent of Europe and in the new American republic, there was an explosion of scientific investigation and invention, accompanied by a growing interest in these matters by the general population.

At the same time, a global private empire had emerged around the British East India Company, that had dominance over trade and finance, based on colonies, plantations, and slave labor. This empire was threatened by the implications of the growth of scientific progress, and its effects on their global system of slavery. It feared the emergence of nation state-republics as vehicles for expanding scientific progress.

This progress would give nations the economic power to resist the empire. But most of all, the spirit of progress itself would ennoble the people, and make them unwilling to accept subservience to any system of tyranny.

How does an empire deal with this, if their leading families and their members are at best amateurs in science? By the 1830s and 1840s there was a desperate sense in Great Britain, the seat of the empire, that all would be lost if no counter could be found to the spirit of scientific optimism. So a new pseudo-science was created to crush this spirit. To accomplish this, they recruited a group of intellectuals from the lower classes who had the drive and the discipline that the leading families and their members lacked. Thomas H. Huxley (1825-1875) was the leader of this group.

Vatican Museum

Huxley's real enemy: Plato

Although Huxley experienced a harsh and impoverished early life, he was inducted into the most prestigious scientific association in Great Britain, the British Royal Society, at the age of twenty-five. This remarkable change of fortune, in a society of rigid class barriers based on birth, attests that Huxley was supported by powerful patrons.

By the time Thomas Huxley was seventeen years of age, he had developed a lacerating, scornful, and sarcastic wit, accompanied by a deep pessimism about the human condition. Unlike his well-educated peers, Huxley had only two years of formal grammar school education. He was apprenticed at age thirteen, and again at fifteen, to two different surgeons. While his age-cohort attended Oxford or Cambridge, Huxley attended to the most impoverished, who were dying of typhoid, venereal disease, malnutrition, and alcoholism in the worst of London's slums. Later, Huxley attended medical school with funds borrowed from his family, showing great promise and winning prizes in Anatomy. However, his poverty prevented him from finishing his education to become a licensed Physician.

In early life, Huxley had developed superb drawing skills, which were useful for making accurate drawings from microscopic observations. This skill enabled him to join the British Navy, as a surgeon's assistant on the research vessel H.M.S. Rattlesnake. His work on drawing newly-discovered sea-organisms off the coast of Australia, as part of the four-year expedition, placed Huxley in the elite of the emerging discipline of Comparative Anatomy.

Upon returning from this expedition, Huxley was allowed to leave the navy, without penalty, long before his term of service ended. Soon after, he became a leading member of Britain's scientific establishment.

Leonard Huxley, Thomas Huxley's son, later recounts in the *Life and Letters of Thomas Huxley*, that his father told him: "Plato was the founder of all the vague and unsound thinking that has burdened philosophy, deserting facts for the possibilities and then, after long and beautiful stories of what might be, telling you he doesn't quite believe them himself. The movement of modern philosophy is back to the position of the old Ionian philosophers, but strengthened and clarified by sound scientific ideas. The thread of philosophical development is not the lines usually laid down for it. It goes from Democritus and the rest to the Epicureans and then to the Stoics, who tried to reconcile it with popular theological ideas."

Huxley was clear that the Empire's real enemy was Plato, and that the Empire needs society's world view to revert to the materialism of Democritus, and the empiricism of Epicurus. Huxley later developed the term "agnosticism" to represent a key aspect of this return to materialism and empiricism.

Thomas Huxley's deeper intention was a revolution against any system of thought which had any trace of Socratic or Platonic thinking, whether in science, religion, culture, or philosophy.

By the 1870s, Huxley had achieved much of this revolution. He was the leader of a small group of nine, who met monthly and called themselves the "X-Club." They took over the institutions of science and education in Great Britain, and later the world.

Change in the Biosphere

In the latter part of the Eighteenth Century, as progress in Science had begun to change the world in a very profound way, discoveries in geology began to contradict the accepted religious view of Creation. Up until this time the strict Biblical view of Creation had never been challenged by science. Leading Geologist Sir Charles Lyell (1797-1875), in his work *Principles of Geology*, established that steady changes were the primary cause of most geological formations. He also showed that these formations developed over very long spans of time, in direct opposition to the interpretations of Scripture.

In efforts to discover the origin and age of formations in geology, discoveries of numerous fossils occurred. Some of these fossils were of biological organisms that no longer existed. This caused great turmoil between science and religion.

In France, Georges Cuvier (1769-1832) and Ettiene Geoffroy Saint Hillaire (1772-1844) were collaborators at the Museum of Natural History in Paris. From their work at the Museum, Cuvier founded the disciplines of Comparative Anatomy and Paleontology, while Geoffroy founded Teratology, the study of animal malformation.

Cuvier argued that the anatomy of an organism of any species is so intricately coordinated functionally and structurally that no part of an organism could change without changing all the other parts of the organism. Such a change of one part by itself would result in the death of the organism. This is known as Cuvier's "correlation of parts" principle.

While Cuvier focused on "correlation of parts," Geoffroy focused on malformations and vestiges in biological organisms. These two areas were viewed by Geoffroy as windows into the inherent potential for change in an organism.

Geoffroy's view differed from Cuvier. For Geoffroy, the anatomy of an organism determined a potential range of function. This range of potential function could be greater or different than the actual functions of an organism. For Geoffroy, the development of an organism's anatomy determined its functional possibilities. Since Geoffroy thought that all animals exhibit the same fundamental plan, or "archetype," he saw no reason why all organisms could not have evolved from a single progenitor.

From the studies of embryos of vertebrates, Geoffroy came up with three parts of his "unity of composition" principle. One was the "law of development," whereby no organ arises or disappears suddenly. This explained vestiges. The second was the "law of compensation," that an organ can grow disproportionately only at the expense of other organs. The third was the "law of relative position," that all the parts of all animals maintain the same positions relative to each other.

These three parts of Geoffroy's "unity of composition" conception suggested that there were coordinated pathways for change within an organism, within certain boundaries of proportion and harmonics.

By the early 1820s, Cuvier and Geoffroy had come into severe disagreement over the origins of anatomical forms. This difference culminated in a historic public debate in 1830. The issues raised in this debate have not been resolved to this day.

Jean Baptiste Lamarck (1744-1829,) a contemporary of Cuvier and Geoffroy, developed the theory that in minor aspects, an organism's adaptation to the environment can be passed on through inheritance. But more importantly, Lamarck was the first to posit that the "principle of life" was the driver of the physical and chemical changes on the Earth, and that these changes were not driven by chemistry or physics as such. In other words, Lamarck viewed the evolution of life not as a "survival of the fittest" response to the environment, but that the "principle of life" is the creator of the physical environment in which living processes further evolve.

By the first part of the 1800s a scientific sense that living processes and their environments "evolve" and change had emerged. The question of how this "evolution" occurred, or could be explained, became the new battleground for conflicting world views.

It was Thomas Huxley's intention to use the conflict between empirical evidence and the strict interpretation of Scriptures to eliminate the influence of Plato. His intention was to impose a bestial conception of man upon humanity through the descent from apes, and to bypass the issues of principle in the Cuvier/Geoffroy debate by focusing attention on an assumed, impossible-to-prove mechanism for evolution: random changes in the small. This mechanism to bypass the issues raised by Cuvier, Geoffroy, and Lamarck was found by Huxley in Charles Darwin's work. It also allowed him to bypass the larger issue of the physical evolution of the earth caused by the evolution of life, which was posed by Lamarck.

Darwin's Controller

Charles Darwin (1809-1882) was one of a number of wealthy heirs to the Wedgewood pottery manufacturing fortune. He was of ill health, and with his fortune he retired to his estate to study biology. In 1838, after reading Thomas Malthus's *On Population*, Darwin formulated a theory of "evolution" based on the "natural selection" of the fittest. Darwin's theories and intentions to publish and promulgate this view of "natural selection" were well-known to an inner group for decades. In the early 1850s Huxley had been introduced to Darwin and by the middle of the 1850s Huxley they were in close collaboration.

While Huxley subsequently became the principal champion of Darwin's theories of evolution by "natural selection," Huxley was well aware of the unscientific nature of Darwin's thesis. Even though Darwin would call Huxley "my bulldog," Huxley, the Comparative Anatomist, had a personal preference for the views of Cuvier on the question of "evolution." Nonetheless Huxley played a leading role in forcing Charles Darwin to publish *Origin of the Species* in 1859.

In a personal letter to his friend and closest collaborator, Joseph Dalton Hooker (1817-1911), dated September 5, 1858, Thomas Huxley exposed something of his intentions for supporting the publication of Darwin's work.

Huxley's protègè Charles Darwin, depicted as "A Venerable Orang-outang," in the satirical magazine The Hornet.

"Wallace's impetus seems to have set Darwin going in earnest, and I am rejoiced to hear we shall learn his views in full, at last. I look forward to a great revolution being effected. Depend upon it, in natural history, and everything else, when the English mind fully determines to work a thing out, it will do it better than any other. I firmly believe in the advent of an English Epoch in science and art, which will lick the Augustan (which, by the bye had neither science nor art in our sense, but you know what I mean) into fits."

Thomas Huxley looked forward to a "great revolution," even though he scientifically disagreed with Darwin's ideas. Huxley's conception was not just a revolution in science, but in art, and culture as well. The issue was "licking the Augustan into fits."

When Huxley wrote this comment to Hooker, although the British Empire ruled most of the world, it did not rule the world of culture. Nor did the empire control the culture internal to Great Britain, which was still influenced by a previous age.

The word Augustan refers to the Augustan Age, the

cultural period of Jonathan Swift, his friend Alexander Pope, and others, whose influence reached far into the Nineteenth Century. The great Swift was a progenitor of the American Revolution; of course his ideas had nothing in common with those Huxley wanted to promote.

The reference that Huxley makes to "Wallace" in the quote refers to Alfred Russell Wallace (1821-1911.) Wallace was an explorer and zoologist, and after a similar encounter with Malthus, had devised a theory of evolution similar to Darwin's. Upon planning to publish his theories before Darwin, numerous men of science intervened to convince Wallace to hold off until Darwin published *Origin of the Species* giving Wallace joint credit. These men felt that Darwin's formulation of "natural selection" and more elaborate supporting biological documentation, were a better vehicle than Wallace's presentation. Also Wallace was not a member of the inner group involved in Huxley's "revolution."

Many have said that Geoffroy's views were the forerunner to Darwin's thesis because they made the idea of "evolution" more respectable. Darwin's views were not similar to Geoffroy's, or Cuvier's or Lamarck's; because they were all looking for a principle, whereas there are no principles in Darwin's theory other than unknowable randomness.

Darwin's ideas of "natural selection" and "survival of the fittest" imply no directionality to evolution. For instance, in Geoffrey's conception, **something** "evolves" out of **something,** which demonstrates a lawful progression or process of some kind. For Geoffroy, "evolution" implies a "plan," a "blueprint" or a "potential" within some "archetypical design."

Rejecting Geoffroy's view that there is such an inherent "potential" in evolution, as Darwin does, creates an insoluble paradox. Either the potential for change is inherent in the organism in which many parts are able to change, in a harmonic or coherent way, or it is not. Any random change of any part by itself will kill the organism.

In today's biology, the complexity of metabolic processes that would have to be changed harmonically would be in the hundreds, if not thousands, of "parts" simultaneously. This would make Darwin's concept of "evolution" impossible.

On the continent of Europe and in the U.S. there was strong opposition to Darwin and Huxley. In the United States one of the leaders who opposed them was the Yale professor and geologist Benjamin Silliman (1779-1864.) His scientific journal, *Journal of American Science and Art* was the principal science publication in America for most of a century, and was known to have corresponded with the *Crelle's Journal* of the European heirs to Leibnitz.

Benjamin Silliman inspired several generations of young scientists. One of these was James Dwight Dana, who also became Silliman's son-in-law and successor as editor of the *Journal of American Science and Art*.

James Dwight Dana, (1813-1895), a contemporary of Thomas Huxley, developed from his own research the view that the directionality of the "evolution" of biological organisms seemed to proceed toward greater "cephalization" (from the Latin indicating "head"). That is, the "evolution" of biological organisms seemed to occur in the direction toward the greater power of the nervous system in animals to respond and interact with the environment. "Evolution," in this way, had a direction toward greater development.

Generally, science outside of Great Britain at this time conceived "evolution" as occurring in a non-random, directed way in which the cognitive powers of humanity represent the pinnacle of the evolutionary process.

To Huxley, this view of humanity was an anathema. It was in this context that he claimed both that all human beings are descended from the apes, and that mankind is in reality just another ape. To this end Thomas Huxley published his *Man's Place in Nature*.

Apex to Ape

It was always Huxley's intention to bring man down to the level of an ape. This was key to extinguishing the optimism in the culture that had emerged from the American Revolution. This was Huxley's most effective and direct attack on the concept that human beings are fundamentally distinct from the animals.

The use of the idea that mankind is descended from the apes biologically, as the core of human identity, has so shaped the modern sense of human identity, in direct opposition to the concept of the human species being distinct from animals, that it is almost impossible for people today to know that they have any identity other than that of an instinct-driven ape-like creature.

Whatever case is made for the anatomical and biological similarity between apes and humans, the species distinction for humans is not biological. Whether or not apes, or any other species going back to some ancient beginning, have or have not some genetic material connection to humanity, is beside the point. What makes us distinctly human is not biology, nor is it biologically determined. The human mind is outside the control of biological processes. Otherwise human will and scientific discoveries would be impossible.

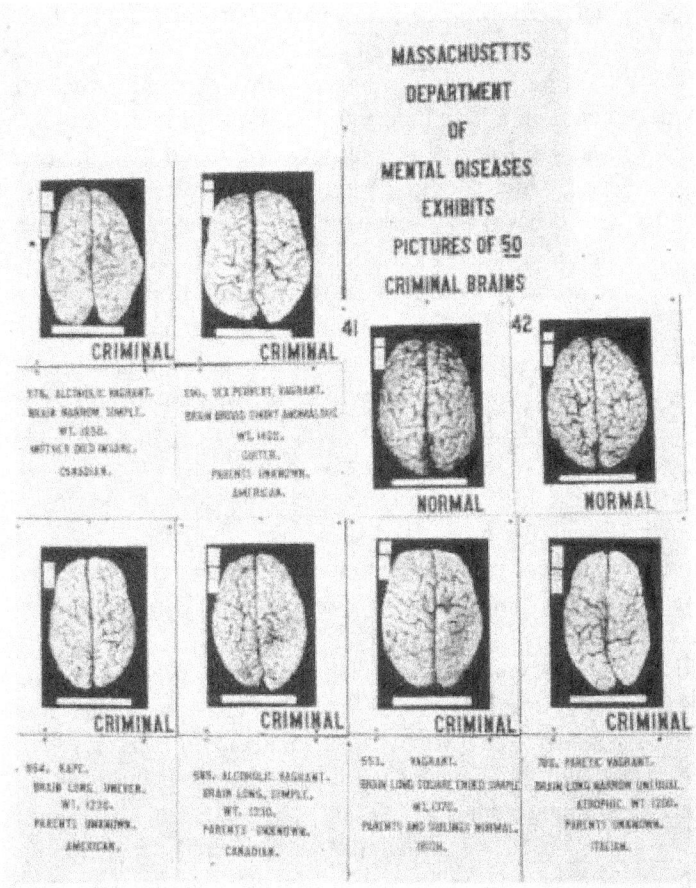

Huxley's outlook on biological determinism spread worldwide.

Huxley's idea came to dominate human identity up to the present day. It became the assumption imbedded in Medicine, Psychology, Biology, Anthropology, and Popular Culture. This includes most emphatically the belief in the biological determinism of human behavior, character, and the potential to learn.

Under Thomas Huxley's influence, the religious and political world increasing split into two groups. Those who found Huxley's bestial views of mankind abhorrent were encouraged to embrace the emerging "Creationist" party. Those who thought "Creationism" could not be sustained by the scientific evidence were encouraged to join Huxley's Darwinian Episcopate. This deep split in society still afflicts us to this day.

American Opposition

Thomas Huxley characterized his opponent, Benjamin Silliman, as the scientist "with one eye on the facts and the other on Genesis." Benjamin Silliman rejected both Darwin and the Creationists.

Instead Silliman emphasized that God's most essential work is being done by mankind through scientific discoveries. He held that while science may contradict one's imperfect understanding of God, it is by man discovering God's universal laws in the physical universe, that mankind is participating in God and is fulfilling God's intention for man, as well as ultimately increasing mankind's understanding of God.

Later when British Prime Minister William Gladstone, on behalf of the Creationists, attacked Darwin and Huxley, Huxley said of Gladstone: "It has always astonished me how a man after fifty or sixty years of life (Gladstone) among men could be so ignorant of the best way to handle his materials. If he had only read Dana, he would have found his case much better stated." Huxley considered Silliman and Dana effective opponents.

With Huxley's "man is an ape" viewpoint, Huxley became the most popular lecturer in what was known as the "workingman's lectures." His lectures on science deeply impacted the Socialists, the Communists, and the Labor Movement, as well as the Anarchists. The cadre of these movements were all indoctrinated into the "materialist ape origins" of the human species. This included Karl Marx and especially Frederick Engels, who totally embraced Huxley and his circle.

At the core of the Communist and Socialist movements, and later the Soviet Union and its cultural catastrophe, lies the spoor of Thomas Huxley. Their vision of a workingman's utopia was strongly laced with the arsenic of Huxley's pessimism about humanity. A utopia which rejects the creative potential of the human species is a hellish place.

The same Darwinian ideas of "evolution" were also at the core of Race Science. Many today would prefer to avoid discussing the fact that their most cherished views on "evolution" were the basis of the Race Science that Hilter practiced.

Huxley led the way by being one of the first to classify the human race into four racial categories; Europeans, Mongolians, Negroes, and Australians. Each category was broken down into sub-categories, and classified according to various attributes, including intelligence. "Natural selection" was used to explain why the European race was superior.

Huxley also took the Darwinian revolution into all the religious institutions, for which he developed the anti-theological term "agnosticism."

Huxley's Darwinian revolution was exported everywhere. His legacy continued into the Twentieth Century through his last major protêgé, H.G. Wells, and his grandsons Aldous and Julian Huxley, who collaborated extensively with Wells.

Darwin's Family Values

The original full title of Darwin's 1859 work is *Origin of the Species by Means of Natural Selection, or Preservation of the Favored Races in the Struggle for Life*. Charles Darwin (1809-1882) in his diary dated October 1838, tells us how he came up with his idea of Natural Selection:

"I happened to read for amusement Malthus *On Population*, and being well prepared to appreciate the struggle for existence which everywhere goes on, from long-continued observation of the habits of animals and plants, it at once struck me that under these circumstances favorable variations would tend to be preserved, and unfavorable ones to be destroyed. The result of this would be the formation of new species. Here, then, I had at least got a theory by which to work."

This entry appears roughly 21 years prior to the publication of Darwin's work. Perhaps Darwin found this section from Malthus amusing:

"All children who are born beyond what would be required to keep up the population to a desired level, must necessarily perish, unless room be made for them by the death of grown persons.... Therefore... we should facilitate, instead of foolishly and vainly endeavoring to impede, the operations of nature in producing this mortality; and if we dread the too frequent visitation of the horrid form of famine, we should sedulously encourage the other forms of destruction, which compel nature to use... Instead of recommending cleanliness to the poor, we should encourage contrary habits... but above all we should reprobate specific remedies for ravaging diseases; and restrain those benevolent, but much mistaken men, who have thought they are doing a service to mankind by protecting schemes for the total extirpation of particular disease." (From *Essay On The Principle Of Population*.)

Today we see the same exact view of Malthus within the British elite publicly exemplified by the likes of Prince Philip, and Prince Charles. Prince Philip's comment that "in the event of being reincarnated, I would like to come back as a deadly virus to deal with the population problem," is a more condensed and pithy version of Malthus. In America this view is most publicly represented by Al Gore, President Barack Obama, and the Green movement.

Charles Darwin was not just one individual who came up with a theory to explain evolution. Rather, he was an instrument of a network, much of it intermarried, which sought to justify mass murder. It is wrong to see Darwin as a scientist. He was complicit, and was, and still is, an instrument for mass murder. What follows is the filling-out of the intermarried network that he was a part of, and which is still active to this day.

Darwin was intimately connected to the Malthusian party of the time, the Whigs. In 1834 the Whigs passed the Poor Laws. At that time, Darwin's dining companion was Harriet Martineau, who many thought would marry Darwin's brother Erasmus. Martineau was the Poor Law propagandist, whose novels helped win the battle for rounding up the poor and incarcerating them in poor-houses, so they would stop having children and be made to work.

Darwin's first cousin and brother-in-law, Hensleigh Wedgwood (1803-1891) was a well-known legal figure and historian, who wrote a book, *On the Origins of Language*, that sought to prove that language evolved from animal grunts.

After Hensleigh's first wife's death, Hensleigh married Fannie or Frances McIntosh, the daughter of Sir James McIntosh.

Sir James McIntosh was the closest friend and collaborator of Thomas Malthus. They both taught at the British East India Company Haileybury College. Fannie, while married to Hensleigh, had an extended affair with Darwin's brother Erasmus.

The next first cousin of Darwin, Sir Francis Galton (1822-1911), founded the eugenics movement. Dalton credited Darwin as the inspiration for the eugenics movement. Galton promoted the idea of culling the "unfit" from the human population. Hitler's racial hygiene policy had its beginnings with these two first cousins, Charles and Francis.

Another of Darwin's first cousins, Sir John Lubbock, banker, biologist, Member of Parliament, extended Darwin's ideas to the study of social institutions and family property. Lubbock developed the concept that inheritable property rights were the highest form of social evolution; that society gradually evolved through stages. The rate of "evolution" in these stages was different for each race. As a member of Huxley's "X-Club," Sir John also played a key political role in this revolution.

Thomas Huxley's closest collaborator and co-founder of the "X-Club" was the botanist Joseph Dalton Hooker (1817-1911.) Hooker and Huxley both become Presidents of the Royal Society in the 1870s, and 1880s. Hooker succeeded his father as the chief Botanist of the Empire.

Hooker is also Darwin's closest friend and collaborator, and is intimately involved in everything Darwin does and writes. Thus Huxley's closest collaborator is Darwin's closest collaborator. Joseph Hooker married Frances Henslow, the daughter of John Stevens Henslow.

John Stevens Henslow (1796-1861), Regis Professor of Botany at Oxford, was both the mentor of Darwin, as well as a tutor to the children of Queen Victoria. It was Darwin's claim that Henslow, the father of his closest collaborator's wife, was also the individual who influenced him the most.

The next major collaborator was Herbert Spencer (1820-1893). Spencer was also a member of Huxley's "X-Club." He was best known for having coined the phrases "survival of the fittest," and "Social Darwinism."

Huxley and Spencer had first met at the salon of Mary Ann Evans (George Eliot) which included Harriet Martineau, John Stuart Mill, and John Chapman, the publisher of the free-trade journal *The Economist*.

Along with Darwin, and Darwin's cousin Sir Francis Galton, Spencer was the major proselytizer of the idea of the innate racial superiority of the upper classes. In Spencer's grand universal scheme, the "fittest" were the socially and economically most successful in society. Spencer espoused the view that the "savage" or inferior races of mankind were the "unfit" and would die out. Spencer was against all charities, child labor laws, women's rights, and the education of the poor. Such measures, Spencer claimed, interfered with the laws of "natural evolution."

By the 1870s, Spencer became the most widely read philosopher in the English speaking world. Spencer's racist views and promotion of "Social Darwinism" had the greatest effect on our culture. It was the popularity of Spencer's promotion of "Social Darwinism" that led to the adoption of a feral competitiveness in our culture.

Herbert Spencer (1820-1903), the popularizer of Social Darwinism.

Competition for wealth, position, and privileges became the dominant driver for one's social sense of self.

As a result, most people today, in their inner sense of identity, are failed persons. Very few reach the pinnacle in the race to the top. Everyone that doesn't, spends their life fantasizing that they had, or worshiping those they think have reached the top. One sees this in Obama's educational policy, "Race To The Top." The sense of social solidarity and the sense of the general welfare of the nation is deeply undermined by this feral competitiveness and this social "survival of the fittest" ideal of Herbert Spencer.

Huxley and Darwin's German collaborator was the zoologist Ernst Haeckel (1834-1919). Haeckel's *The History of Creation* was the most-read book in the world explaining Darwin's ideas scientifically. Haeckel also founded the discipline of Ecology. He was the first to develop concepts of "overpopulation" and "carrying capacity." Haeckel also promoted the notion that the social sciences should be governed by the discipline of "Applied Biology." "Applied Biology" was Haeckel's term for eugenics.

Among Huxley's and Darwin's group of scientists, there were two who eventually dissented. One of these was the explorer and zoologist Alfred Russell Wallace. The other was the geologist Sir Charles Lyell.

Wallace was the "co-discoverer" of the principle of "natural selection" with Darwin. By 1864, Wallace had come into disagreement with Darwin and Huxley. Wallace had reached the conclusion that the evolution of matter in the universe could not have occurred in a gradual, or "natural selection" manner in three very critical instances.

One of these instances was the transition from inorganic to biological matter. The second was the transition from biological matter to the existence of consciousness in higher animals. The third was the transition from higher animals' sense of consciousness to the ability to reason in mankind. To Wallace these three leaps could not be explained by Darwin's theories. Eventually, Wallace become convinced that something "outside"; something "spiritual" had to have in-

Sir Charles Lyell (left) and Sir Richard Owen (right), two of Darwin's scientific opponents.

tervened to cause these leaps. This issue ultimately led Wallace to turn to spiritualism.

Sir Charles Lyell had been a collaborator of Darwin since 1837. Lyell was also a friend and early promoter of Huxley. Nonetheless, Lyell had become very concerned that Darwin and Huxley were using "gradualist" evolutionary ideas to promote a "catastrophic criminal view of mankind." Lyell strongly believed that human beings possessed faculties of reason that in no way could have emerged from Darwin's "natural selection."

Another contemporary of Darwin and Huxley, who had initially helped to promote Huxley into the Royal Society was Sir Richard Owen (1804-1892.) Huxley and Owen would engage in a bitter struggle over fundamental issues of science and evolution which lasted 40 years. Owen adopted the view of "archetypes" as opposed to "natural selection." Since "archetypes" were seen as showing God's design, the battle of "archetypes" versus "natural selection" became in essence the battle of the Church of England versus the British East India Company crowd. Owen would later call Huxley a "pervert with some perhaps congenital defect of mind for denying the divine in Nature."

Twentieth-Century Eugenics

The transition from Darwin and Huxley to the next generation, was marked by a change from "theory" to "practice." The theories that were developed in the Malthusian Darwinian revolution, such as "natural selection," "survival of the fittest," the "descent of man from the apes," and "eugenics," gave way to the preparations for the mass murder of those deemed "unfit."

The most notable son of Charles Darwin was Leonard Darwin (1850-1943). Leonard became the President of the British Eugenics society (1911-1928), succeeding his father's cousin Francis Galton.

Leonard Darwin's most important successor was Ronald A. Fisher (1890-1962), who pioneered the study of statistics in genetics on which modern Darwinism was based. Fisher was notorious for refusing to shift away from his racist and eugenicist views after the defeat of Hitler. The modern Darwinopath, Richard Dawkins, claimed that Ronald Fisher was the "greatest of Darwin's successors."

Another son of Darwin was Horace Darwin. Horace was the co-founder, with Ronald Fisher and John Maynard Keynes, of the Cambridge Eugenics Society.

So here we have two of Darwin's sons leading the way to establish the means to "cull" the human species of the "unfit." Who are the "unfit?" The "unfit" are you, me, most of the human race, and any person or group so deemed.

A key leader in the third generation of Malthus' Darwinian revolution was Darwin's grandson, Charles Galton Darwin (1887-1962.) Charles Galton Darwin was the leading British physicist during World War II. He ran Britain's National Laboratories and led the British side of the Manhattan Atomic Bomb Project. After World War II, Charles retired to direct the British Eugenics Society until his death in 1962. Charles Galton Darwin was also the godson of Sir Francis Galton.

In 1952, Charles Galton Darwin published *The Next Million Years* as his contribution to furthering eugenics and the Darwinian revolution. *The Next Million Years* recast the issue of eugenics not in terms of racial hygiene, but in terms of curbing population growth. Charles estimated that the time it would take for mankind to biologically evolve into a new species would be a million years. In the meantime, Charles said that the principal problem was that human beings were essentially "wild animals" that had not been domesticated, although he believed every effort should be made to do so.

It was the British Eugenics Society and its American

extension which launched the Hastings Center on Euthanasia in the United Statesin the 1960s. It was the Hastings Center and its leading operative, Ezekiel Emmanuel, who crafted Obama's Health Care Reform to "cull" the "poor" and the "elderly," and relieve society of the financial burden of the "unfit."

The granddaughter of Charles Darwin, Charles Galton Darwin's sister Margaret, married Geoffrey Keynes, the brother of John Maynard Keynes. The great-grandson of Charles Darwin, and son of Charles Galton Darwin, George Pember Darwin (1928-2001) married Angela Huxley, the great-grand-daughter of Thomas Huxley.

And so it goes.

Evolution of Genocide

In Germany, the second generation of Darwinians was led by leaders such as Alfred Ploetz (1860-1940). Ploetz was an ardent follower of both Darwin and Haeckel, and became a leading member of the British Eugenics Society. He toured the United States extensively to popularize the eugenics movement in America. Ploetz was the first to name and develop the "branch of medicine" called "racial hygiene." On returning to Germany in 1936, Ploetz, with his brother-in-law and protégé Ernst Rudin, was appointed by Adolph Hitler to oversee the justification of mass murder based on "racial hygiene."

One of the leading promoters of eugenics in the more recent period was Sir Crispin Tickell. Sir Crispin was the President of the Royal Geographical Society and a leading government official and adviser to Prime Minister Margaret Thatcher. In the 1980s, Sir Crispin created the British Government-funded "climate change " movement to implement mass murder based on reducing carbon dioxide emissions. Sir Crispin Tickell's great-grand-father was Thomas Huxley.

And so it goes on, generation after generation, of policies intended to cause mass genocide.

By the year 1900, Darwinism was on the wane in the scientific community. It lacked the experimental proof that it needed to justify its tenets. Darwinism was under attack from many quarters. It lacked most of all, some discovery of an intermediate form, or "missing link" between man and ape.

At last this "missing evidence" came in the form of the discovery at Piltdown, where the jaw of an ape was fused with the cranium of a human. Even this fabricated

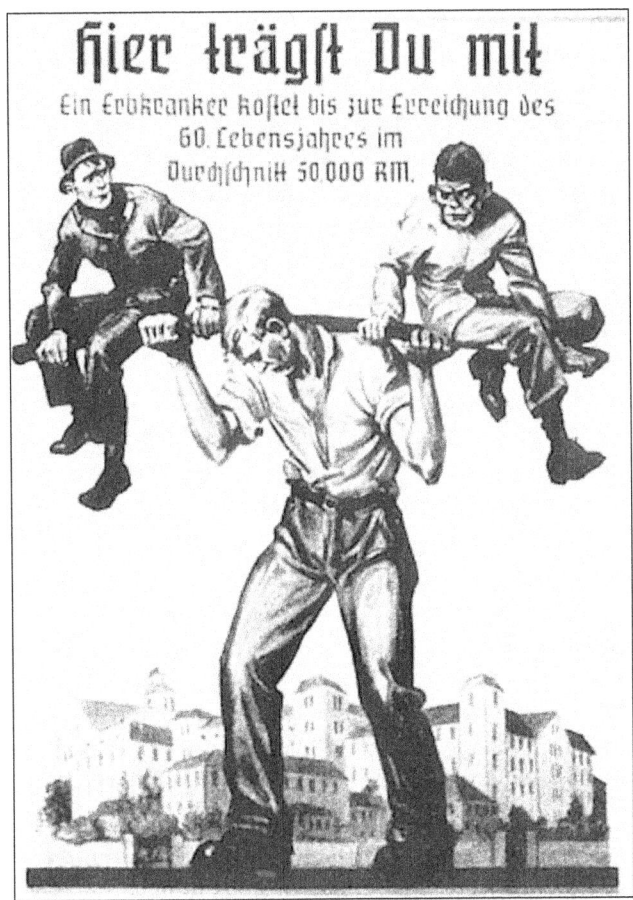

Shown, a sample of pre-Nazi German Malthusian propaganda: "Look who you're carrying. One person with birth defects over 60 years old costs an average of 50,000 Reichsmarks."

link between man and ape, could not stem the erosion of Darwin's influence in the scientific community during the 1920s and 1930s. The fossil evidence did not exist to support the theory of "natural selection."

The fossil evidence to support Darwin does not exist to this day!

It fell to Huxley's grandson, zoologist Julian Huxley to come to the rescue of the Darwinian revolution. Early in Julian Huxley's career, Julian had replaced Leonard Darwin as head of the British Eugenics Society. With the help of Thomas Huxley's last major protégé, H.G. Wells, Julian Huxley launched a revival of Darwinism. This revival was named the "evolutionary synthesis," or the "new synthesis," or the "modern synthesis."

Under Julian Huxley's direction, a number of disciplines were merged. These were biochemistry, genetics, population studies, and ecological field studies. By merging these disciplines, a new model was created that no longer needed the intermediate fossil evidence. In the "new synthesis," the human "animal" was governed by biochemical and genetically determined processes down to the predisposition in all areas of behavior, intelligence, disease, sexual preferences, even altruism.

The bases of the "new synthesis" are as follows: The genes or the DNA are continuously impacted by background radiation and other factors which cause mutation, or small changes in the DNA, and its sequences. This is called "genetic drift." This "genetic drift" is supposedly constant. The DNA is supposed to be the blueprint that passes on inherited characteristics. Then the environment acts on these inherited changes in the organism, and selects out those changes that benefit the survival of individual organisms. Over time this leads to new species and evolution.

Also involved is the concept of "gene pool." If a group of organisms of one species become isolated geographically from others of the same species, the isolated part will tend to develop a separate "gene pool," and there would be a more rapid rate of differentiation between the two populations. The "new synthesis" like the older version of "natural selection" has no directionality. The driver for the "new synthesis" is random changes in the small caused by the impact of background radiation.

H.G. Wells and Julian Huxley collaborated in producing a very popular 1500 page book in 1939, *The Science of Life*. This book was what began the popular revival of Darwin in the population. The last paragraph of the "Science of Ecology" section on page 1011 stated: "Unrestrained breeding, for man and animals alike, whether they are mice, lemmings, locusts, Italians, Hindoos, or Chinamen, is biologically a thoroughly evil thing."

To Make All Agnostics

The Darwinian revolution also infected other areas and disciplines. Two developments of importance occurred in the 1860s in the "procession through the institutions" of Huxley's group of associates. One was the founding of the "X Club" with nine members. The second was the formation of The Metaphysical Society (1869-1880).

The "X Club" sponsored and launched two press organs to support their revolution. One was the *Weekly Reader*, and the other was *Natural History Review* of which Huxley was part owner. Both these publications were used in the early 1860s to promote the pro-Dar-

winian view. Thomas Huxley was the leading editor and polemicist in these publications. But both publications failed, and were replaced by a fully "X-Club"-backed publication that was launched in 1869 called *Nature*.

Nature is still in existence.

The other institution Huxley formed, the Metaphysical Society, brought together the most prominent men of science, religion, culture, and philosophy to a monthly dinner and discussion. The purpose of the Society was to meet and discuss fundamental issues such as "Is God knowable?" or "What is a Lie?," or "The Ethics of Belief," or "What Is Death?" Present were leading clerics, writers, philosophers, politicians, and scientists. Among the rotating chairmen were Thomas Huxley, Sir John Lubbock, and William Gladstone, the Prime Minister of Great Britain.

From eye-witness descriptions, everyone was cordial, and the discussions would generally come down to Huxley demonstrating that "the working hypothesis of science" laboring gradually over the years through empirical work, was far superior to all the metaphysical speculation about anything. God was empirically unknowable.

At an early age Thomas Huxley's interest in Philosophy had led him study Emmanuel Kant in German. Huxley had also become a convert to the Scottish philosopher Sir William Hamilton (1788-1856). Both Kant and Hamilton maintained that God was unknowable. Based on the proposition of the unknowability of God, Huxley launched a movement in philosophy, religion, and science which he termed "agnosticism." The aim of this movement was to eliminate anything that is Platonic or metaphysical in science. Huxley's "agnosticism" became the governing ideology, or the new "religion" of the empire.

This new "religion" of "agnosticism" was not to be for the masses. This was the new "religion" of the functionaries of the empire; the "scientists," the "academics," and the enlightened "liberal clerics." As for the masses, they would be given all the "irrational feelings" and "beliefs" they would want, but not the knowledge of universal principles.

In an "agnostically" administered empire, the masses can kill each other in perpetual conflict over "their" religious feelings.

Under Huxley's "agnostic" Darwinian episcopate, a person of science can not assert the truthfulness of the existence of God. Nor can a person of science assert conversely that God does not exist. Both assertions maintain that human beings have a capacity to know, whereas an "agnostic" can not know,— and by not knowing has no responsibility for mankind or the future.

So what can be proven, as far as fundamental principles involving the lawfulness of the universe, according to the "agnosticism" which now rules the sciences? Nothing! So what is left? What is left is statistics! "We don't know anything but statistical probabilities." In the agnosticism of "modern science," there is no causality other than the "bumping" into each other of "things" in ways we can never fully understand, other than they are "bumping" into each other.

Thomas Huxley at the blackboard.

What about Darwinism? It's the same thing! Random mutations in ways we can never know create "statistical probabilities" for increased survival for "random" changes caused by "random" events. In other words, human beings are unable to know the existence of any real causation, just statistics. Or to put it in another way, the lawfulness or unlawfulness of the Universe is unknowable to the human species. All we can know is our "bumping" into "things."

But the universe is not governed by statistically random processes! To believe so is to believe in the irrational. Not knowing the causes of things does not make them random. To substitute randomness for causality is not just unscientific—it is insane. How is it possible to discover the science behind evolution, if anything but randomness as an explanation is outlawed?

The real issue and the truths behind the revolution of Darwin and Huxley were political. Neither Thomas Huxley, nor his grandson Julian Huxley cared much for whether there was any truth in Darwin's theories. The issue for them was never truth, or science. The issue for them was who was going to control the ideas that govern the thinking of those who influence and run so-

ciety! The issue was who would control "science," and for whom. Without the Darwinian-Huxley revolution in the sciences, the empire of Malthusian genocide would have been defeated long ago. We would now be colonizing the solar system instead of entering a Dark Age collapse of civilization.

The scientific truth of evolution and how it takes place is not yet known. What we do know is that it cannot be random. We know this because we are human beings, and we make plans for the future, and we are not random in our actions. In this age, the essence of being human is to wage war against this hideous revolution and recover the lost promise of the potential of our species.

Sources

Huxley, Leonard: *Life and Letters of Thomas Henry Huxley*, Vol. I, Appleton, 1902.

Morris, Desmond: *From Devil's Disciple to Evolution's High Priest*, Reading, Mass., Addison-Wesley, 1997.

Lyons, Sherrie L: *Thomas Henry Huxley, The Evolution of a Scientist*, Prometheus Books, 2000.

Fulton, John F. and Thompson, Elizabeth H.: *Benjamin Silliman, Pathfinder in American Science*, Yale U. School of Medicine, 1947

Prince Phillip's Radio Address in the 1980s in Germany.

Hutton, R.H.: *Accounts of 1885 Metaphysical Society Meetings*.

Blinderman, Charles: *The Piltdown Inquest*, Prometheus Books, 1986.

Wells, H.G. and Huxley, Julian S.: *The Science of Life*, Garden City Publishing Co, Inc., 1939.

Further Reading

Ross, Jason: "Evolution and Organismic Communication," Research Report, July 26, 2010.

Carol Hugunin, "Let's Bury Darwin," *21st Century Science and Technology*, Spring 1995.

The Ouster of Bismarck and The Start of World War I

by Jeffrey Steinberg

June 8—To be true to history, it must be said that the forced resignation of Otto von Bismarck (1815-1898) as Chancellor of Germany on March 20, 1890 marks the true starting date of what came to be known as World War I. For nearly 30 years, Bismarck had conducted the most profound diplomacy in modern European history, engineering the creation of a unified German state, forging an alliance with the United States, and conducting a foreign policy of war-avoidance on the European continent, while holding England and France in check, to prevent their intervention in North America on behalf of the Confederacy.

One of the most underrated features of Bismarck's rise and success was his deep collaboration, dating from his university days at Göttingen and Berlin, with a group of American diplomats and political economists, who saw, in the creation of a unified German nation-state, the spreading of the American republican principles and the American System of Political Economy into continental Europe, after the failure of the French Revolution and the ensuing Napoleonic Wars and the disastrous Congress of Vienna. Among the crowning accomplishments of that Congress was the prevention of the emergence of a unified Germany, maintaining, instead, a collection of 36 separate principalities, aligned with the Austro-Hungarian Empire.

Otto von Bismarck in 1880.

The American System

Before there was Otto von Bismarck, there was Friedrich List (1789-1846). As the result of political intrigues in his native Württemberg, List migrated to the United States in 1824, where he remained for the next eight years, eventually obtaining American citizenship. List settled in Reading, Pa., founded a German-English-language newspaper, and became a strong advocate of railroad construction and other vital infrastructure programs. In 1827, List wrote his first major work, *Outlines on American Political Economy*.

List had studied the reports to Congress of America's first Secretary of the Treasury, Alexander Hamilton, and became a powerful advocate of Hamiltonian economics, developing the concept of "capital of mind" throughout his writings. By this, he meant the power of human creativity to invent and engage in the advancement of society as a whole. This concept required the organization of nation-states, which he also described as the "confederation of productive forces."

In 1832, List returned to Europe, as the American Consul in Hamburg, and later in Leipzig. Back in Europe, List wrote his two other major works, *The Natural System of Political Economy* (1837), and *The National System of Political Economy* (1841). In Leipzig, he took a leading role in promoting the integration of a

The German Post Office's stamp commemorating the "father of the German Railways," the German-American economist Friedrich List.

German railroad system. In 1846, he wrote a proposal, published in the *Eisenbahn Journal*, titled "The Railway Line from Ostende to Bombay," which, in reality, was the seed idea for his later plans for a Eurasian rail system linking continental Western Europe to China. He wrote:

> People should realize that the distance from Ostende [Belgium] to Bombay [India] could be covered in 10 days. A steamship will need 40 days, a clipper will take 100 to 120 days. So people should realize the great economic advantage of going to such a Eurasian railway line.

Not surprisingly, during this period, List came under vicious attack from the London *Economist* and the London *Times*, already two flagship publications of the British Empire. The *Economist* described List as a great agitator" whose system "is a cry for protective duties, this naked selfishness ... built on lies and sophisms, denying the experience of centuries.

Shortly before his untimely death in 1846, List visited London, where he met with Prince Albert, the Royal Consort and husband of Queen Victoria; Viscount Palmerston; and Sir Robert Peel. He presented them with a memorandum, "Politics of the Future," which was one of the most prescient assessments of the global strategic situation of the period. He wrote:

> The days are numbered in which Britain will be able to preserve its global economic and trade supremacy. Already now, the United States of America are passing Britain in economic and trade power. The productive forces of the U.S. are growing geometrically, the British are growing only arithmetically. The time of British supremacy on the sea, and in world trade, is coming to an end, and Britain has only two choices. Number one, a war against the United States, leading to the dismemberment of the United States; or secondly, a radical change in Britain's economic policy, turning away from free trade, and accepting protectionism as the natural way for other nations to develop economically, and understanding that protectionism does not contain the volume of trade, as protectionism allows internal economic development; in spite of protectionism, the volume of trade will grow. Britain can only have a future, if it realizes the significance of the two new revolutionary means of communication, number one, railway, and number two, the telegraph, the electric telegraph. A key aspect for Britain, given its vast reservoir of capital, would be not only to accept but to support the project of a European-Asiatic Railway line, comparable to what the United States is presently committed to, the project of a railway connection between the Atlantic Coast and the Pacific Coast, as well as the coast of the Gulf of Mexico.

List returned from that six-week visit to England a physical and psychological wreck, and he was dead three months later, ostensibly by suicide.

Bismarck and the Unification of Germany

The great Russian diplomat and physical economist Count Sergei Witte has been cited as stating that Otto von Bismarck had a copy of List's *National System of Political Economy* on his bed table throughout his time in office.

What is certain, is that Bismarck became a devoted follower of List and the American System of Political Economy, backing List's plan for the creation of a German Customs Union as a crucial step towards national integration, and engineering a shift in Germany from free trade to protectionism in 1878-79.

All the while, Bismarck maintained a global view of

diplomacy, maneuvering to sever the German principalities from the Austro-Hungarian Empire, maintaining good Prussian diplomatic ties with Russia, and averting any provocations toward France or Britain that could lead to a European war, while he moved Germany, step by step, toward the goal of national integration.

Bismarck's exposure to the American System did not exclusively come from his studies of List. As a university student at Göttingen and Berlin, he became a close friend of John Lothrop Motley, and the Bismarck-Motley personal tie would last for decades, as Bismarck became the head of state of Prussia, and later of a unified Germany, and Motley became U.S. Ambassador to Britain and the Austro-Hungarian Empire.

Motley came from a revolutionary New England family, and he and other American republicans were part of a network of scholar/diplomats who studied in the great German universities and remained in Europe as leading American diplomats. Among the circle were both Motley and George Bancroft, who was U.S. Ambassador to Berlin from 1867-1874.

Motley was a frequent guest of Bismarck, as the Prussian leader moved toward liberating all of Germany from the grip of the Austro-Hungarians and French, who were both operating under the overall domination of Europe by Britain.

In June 1859, after several recent visits with Bismarck, Motley wrote to his mother:

> If there were a young, vigorous, intellectual sovereign in Prussia at this moment, a man like Frederic the Great or Peter the Great, he would see that the time has arrived for Prussia to secure at last the object of its ambition, the imperial crown of Germany. If the House of Brandenburg which governs the powerful, wholly German and progressive Prussia, could become Emperors of Germany, to the utter annihilation of a fictitious, artificial sham, which [was] got up at the Congress of Vienna 50 years ago, and baptized the Empire of Austria, in which there are only about 7 million Germans, shaken up pell-mell in a great bag with 30 millions of Slavonians, Magyars, Italians, Croats, and Greeks, and Lord knows what hodge-podge, which has never had any vitality except in defiance of all laws, divine or human—if such a result could take place, then

there might be a real Germany, and a handsome solution to the present European question.

When Motley wrote this letter, he was well-informed of his friend Bismarck's Grand Plan for a unified Germany. At the time, Bismarck was Prussian Ambassador to Russia, and he would later serve in the same posting in Paris. In October 1862, Bismarck was appointed as Minister President of Prussia. He would remain in that post and the successive post of Chancellor of Germany for the next 28 years. During that time, he engineered three limited military operations, all aimed at achieving consolidation of a unified Germany. In 1863, he secured the independence of Schleswig and Holstein from Denmark. In the Summer of 1866, he allied with Sardinia in a brief war with Austria, which resulted in the German takeover of both states. In 1870, he engineered a similar brief war with France, which consolidated the southern German states of Bavaria, Württemberg, Baden, and Southern Hesse.

In the treaty that concluded the conflict with France, Germany also took control over Alsace and Lorraine. On Jan. 18, 1871, the Prussian-dominated North German Confederation was superceded by the establishment of a unified German state. Bismarck was named by King Wilhelm I as Reichskanzler.

Bismarck's military/diplomatic outlook was trans-Atlantic in scope. Even as he was consolidating the establishment of a unified German nation, he was providing vital assistance to President Lincoln against Britain and France, who were seeking every opportunity to enter the American Civil War in support of the Confederacy. Not only did his military actions pin down European rivals and block them from taking a more active role in the Civil War, he also encouraged German banks to purchase American war bonds, thus providing a crucial source of funding for Lincoln.

Motley wrote to Bismarck, reflecting on the trans-Atlantic situation:

> I presume if the Great Powers of Europe are drawn into a war on the Schleswig-Holstein question, we shall not be any longer taunted with urging war.... France would like to fight Prussia, and get the Rhine provinces, but England could not stand that, nor Austria either, much as she hates Prussia.

Bismarck wrote back to Motley on May 23, 1864, asking his American friend to visit him, adding:

> I promise that the Union flag shall wave over our house and conversation and the best old hock shall pour damnation over the rebels.

Having succeeded in unifying Germany, independent of the Austro-Hungarian Empire, Bismarck spent the next years transforming German policy to the American System. In this fight, he had key allies, most significantly, Wilhelm von Kardorff, a member of the Reichstag, who was a close ally of Bismarck's economic advisor and personal banker, Gerson von Bleichröder. Von Kardorff would found the Confederation of German Industry and serve as its first president in 1876. From that position, he strongly urged Bismarck to adopt protectionist policies.

In May 1879, Bismarck delivered a speech before the Reichstag, announcing a new economic direction for Germany:

> Our previous open-door policies made us a dumping ground for the excess production of other countries. In my view, this drove prices in Germany through the floor. That prevented the growth of our industries and the development of our economic life. We must close this door, and erect a higher barrier. And what I propose now, is that we create the same market for German industry which previously, out of the goodness of our hearts, we allowed foreigners to exploit. If the danger of protectionism were as great as the advocates of free trade claim, then France would long ago have become impoverished, since it has adhered to this theory since the times of Colbert.

By July 1879, Bismarck had nationalized the railroads under the newly established Ministry for Public Affairs. He instituted the most advanced social welfare programs in the world, and made other revolutionary reforms based on the general welfare, which surpassed even those enacted in the United States.

Britain's War Against the Land-Bridge

The dominant figure in Britain throughout the Victorian era, was the Queen's son Prince Edward

Britain's King Edward VII in his coronation robes.

Albert, later, King Edward VII. His hatred for Bismarck and Germany was profound, and he held Bismarck responsible for Lincoln's victory in the Civil War, among other crimes against the Empire. But so long as Kaiser Wilhelm I remained on the throne of the newly established German Empire, Britain was stymied.

Everything changed in March 1888, when Kaiser Wilhelm I died at the age of 91, and was replaced by his son Frederic, who was, however, already terminally ill, and would die in June. Frederic's oldest son, Wilhelm, succeeded to the throne as Wilhelm II.

Wilhelm II was jealous of Bismarck's power, and was an easy pawn for Edward Albert's manipulations (all of the major European monarchs were blood relatives of Queen Victoria). After a number of disputes, Wilhelm II demanded Bismarck's resignation on March 18, 1890.

Shortly before his death on July 28, 1898, Bismarck warned of a coming war in Europe, declaring:

> If ever there was to be another war in Europe, it will come out of some damned silly thing in the Balkans.

He viewed the 29-year-old new Kaiser as an impetuous war-monger who would soon break Bismarck's carefully devised collaboration with Russia, by seeking confrontation. Bismarck was absolutely right.

Bismarck was, furthermore, well aware of the British intrigues to keep Germany out of the Russian-German-French anti-war alliance that had been promoted by both Witte and French Foreign Minister Gabriel Hanotaux, following Bismarck's ouster. The idea of such a tripartite anti-British alliance had been at the heart of Bismarck's own continental diplomacy, which aimed to assure Russia that there would be no German support for any Austro-Hungarian machinations against Russia. Without that German support, a fragile peace was maintained on the European continent, which not only lasted for decades, but allowed for the development of ambitious railroad projects, from the Berlin-to-Baghdad Rail, to the Trans-Siberian Railroad.

Kaiser Wilhelm II, for all practical purposes, a dupe of Prince Edward Albert, was manipulated into keeping Germany out of the durable alliance with France and Russia that was in Germany's actual vital interest.

Edward Albert (later King Edward VII) devoted all of his efforts toward isolating and encircling Germany. To this end, he manipulated a series of "little wars" throughout Eurasia, from the Balkans to the Far East. Robert Blatchford wrote in the *Daily Mail* of Dec. 14, 1909:

> …the king and his counselors have strained every nerve to establish ententes with Russia and with Italy; and have formed an entente with France, and as well with Japan. Why? To isolate Germany.

For a fleeting moment on the eve of the formal outbreak of World War I in August 1914, Kaiser Wilhelm II realized what Bismarck had warned of. The Kaiser wrote:

> England, Russia, and France have agreed among themselves … after laying the foundation of the *casus foederis* for us through Austria … to take the Austro-Serbian conflict for an excuse for waging a war of extermination against us…. That is the real naked situation slowly and cleverly set going by Edward VII and … finally brought to a conclusion by George V…. So the famous encirclement of Germany has finally become a fact, despite every effort of our politicians and diplomats to prevent it. The net has suddenly been thrown over our head, and England sneeringly reaps the most brilliant success of her persistently prosecuted purely anti-German world policy against which we have proved ourselves helpless, while she twists the noose of our political and economic destruction out of our fidelity to Austria, as we squirm isolated in the nest.

The firing of Bismarck, who anchored continental European peace and stability on a war-prevention alliance with Russia, and who had played a masterful strategic war against Britain on both sides of the Atlantic, was truly the first shot of a century of war.

London's Murder of McKinley Launched a Century of Assassinations

by Jeffrey Steinberg and Anton Chaitkin

June 9—President William McKinley (1843-1901) was the last American President to have fought for the Union in the Civil War. He was the last of the Republican Party protectionists, and the last self-conscious proponent of the Hamiltonian American System of Political Economy.

McKinley's assassination on Sept. 6, 1901, less than six months after he was inaugurated for his second term as President of the United States, was a turning point in American history. McKinley's assassination brought Theodore Roosevelt into the Presidency, and ushered in a century of Anglo-American collusion, all to the detriment of the nation and the world.

McKinley's assassination also launched what can be fairly called a Century of Assassinations. Every outstanding American president of the Twentieth Century would be targeted for assassination, and in every instance, the evidence would lead to one and only one institution: The British Monarchy.

In the Cross-Hairs

President Franklin Roosevelt was targeted by the British and their Wall Street allies for assassination, even before his inauguration.[1] When the assassination attempt failed, Wall Street and London financed an attempted coup against FDR, which was thwarted by Gen. Smedley Butler, who blew the whistle on the plot which had been organized out of the Wall Street and London offices of JP Morgan.

John F. Kennedy was assassinated on Nov. 22, 1963 by an elaborate conspiracy that the late New Orleans District Attorney Jim Garrison traced, through Montreal, Canada, to a British intelligence front company, Permindex, which also financed repeated assassination attempts against French President Charles de Gaulle.

Library of Congress

President William McKinley gives his Inaugural address, March 4, 1897.

President Ronald Reagan was the victim of a nearly-successful assassination attempt within his first months in office. The parallels between the McKinley and Reagan assassination attempts are striking: Both McKinley and Reagan came under pressure from Wall Street factions of their own Republican Party to name known British sympathizers as their vice presidential running mates.

McKinley's assassination installed TR in the White House, and the failed assassination attempt against Reagan, which greatly weakened him, opened the door for George H.W. Bush to assume more and more Executive authorities, leading to his own one-term Presidency and the later election of his son, George W. Bush.

President Bill Clinton, who singled himself out as a dissenter from the Anglo-American "Special Relation-

---

1. Steinberg, Jeffrey. "FDR's 1932 Victory Over Lond's Wall Street Fascists," *EIR*, April 4, 2008.

ship," and sought to replace it with a strategic partnership with Germany, under Chancellors Helmut Kohl and Gerhard Schroeder, was stalked by British agents, led by MI6 asset Ambrose Evans-Pritchard. When private airplanes were not crashing into the White House residency, British propagandists, led by Evans-Pritchard, were instigating rightwing militia violence against the President, and pressing Republicans in Congress to bring down his Presidency via impeachment.

President Clinton was betrayed by his own Vice President, Albert Gore, a close collaborator of British Royal Consort and notorious genocidalist, Prince Philip, who attempted to use the "Lewinsky affair" to force Clinton's resignation.

President Clinton was in the process of launching a "new global financial architecture," following the financial crisis of 1997-1998, and was brought down because of his plans to overhaul the British system of speculative finance.

American Presidents were not the only leading American patriots who were targets of British-engineered assassins. Rev. Martin Luther King Jr. was gunned down in 1968 at the point that he was broadening the agenda of the already powerful civil rights movement; and shortly after the MLK assassination, Robert F. Kennedy, the brother of the slain JFK and the leading Democratic Party candidate for the 1968 presidential nomination, was assassinated during a campaign appearance in Los Angeles.

The McKinley Assassination

William McKinley was a leading American protectionist, who served in the U.S. Congress and as Governor of Ohio, before being elected President in 1896.

In 1882, McKinley, then a Republican Congressman from Ohio, delivered a powerful rebuke of free trade on the floor of the House of Representatives. Noting that there was no American support for free trade, he asked, rhetorically, who did favor free trade? "England wants it, demands it—not for our good but for hers; for she is more anxious to maintain her old position of supremacy than she is to promote the interests and welfare of the people of this republic, and a great party in this country voices her interest.... She would manufacture for us, and permit us to raise wheat and corn for her. We are satisfied to do the latter, but unwilling to concede to her the monopoly of the former."

McKinley polemicised:

President Theodore Roosevelt.

Free trade may be suitable to Great Britain and its peculiar social and political structure, but it has no place in this republic, where classes are unknown, and where caste has long since been banished; where equality is a rule; where labor is dignified and honorable; where education and improvement are the individual striving of every citizen, no matter what may be the accident of his birth, or the poverty of his early surroundings. Here the mechanic of today is the manufacturer of a few years hence. Under such conditions, free trade can have no abiding place here.

True to his words, McKinley pushed through a tariff law, the McKinley Tariff, in 1890, which was augmented by then-Secretary of State James Blaine, who initiated treaties of "reciprocity" with countries of South America and Mexico, to enhance trade, while maintaining common protection against Britain's free trade policies.

The British diplomat Sir Cecil Spring-Rice wrote back to London that the combined impact of the McKinley Tariff and Blaine's reciprocity policy, effectively shut Britain out of the entirety of the West Indies and South America. Within a few years, Spring-Rice would be an intimate of Theodore Roosevelt.

Roosevelt was already an unabashed Anglophile, a trait he inherited from his "favorite uncle," James D. Bulloch, who ran the Confederate intelligence services out of London throughout the Civil War. In 1883, Bulloch published his Civil War espionage history, *The Secret Service of the Confederate States in Europe*. Bulloch was directly implicated in the Lincoln assassination, through his pivotal role as liaison between the British intelligence services and the Confederacy.

McKinley posed a threat to British interests, and he was targeted for assassination for that crime against the Crown. But first, a proper successor to the Presidency had to be put in place.

When his vice president in his first term, Garrett Hobart, died in 1899, McKinley came under intense pressure from the Wall Street, pro-British faction of his own Republican Party to name TR as his Vice President. He and his closest political advisor, Sen. Marcus Alonzo Hanna, capitulated to the pressure and named Roosevelt to the ticket.

President McKinley was re-elected in 1900. He understood that he was a target of assassination, and his chief aide, Sen. Hanna, had written a memo, demanding that "proper safeguards be thrown around the person of the President." The memo reported that the U.S. government had been informed that

> anarchists or Socialists through their various organizations resolved to rid the earth of a number of its rulers [starting with] the Empress Eugenie of Austria ... the King of Italy ... [and] then the President of the United States ... and the first two calls ... have come to pass as predicted.

The New York Police Department was aware, and warned McKinley that the Henry Street Settlement House was a hotbed of anarchist activity, and would be the location from which an assassination attempt against the President would most likely be launched.

During a visit to Buffalo, New York, McKinley was fatally shot by anarchist Leon Czolgosz, a disciple of Emma Goldman. Czolgosz confessed to having heard a Goldman lecture weeks before the killing, calling for

White House/Ralph Alswang

President William J. Clinton, target of British political assassination, at a White House Interfaith Breakfast.

the destruction of the American government. Goldman was temporarily arrested on charges of complicity in the McKinley assassination, but was later released.

But the real story behind Henry Street and the London-centered Fabian movement behind the New York anarchist safehouse traced directly to the British Crown. Henry Street Settlement House had been financed by Wall Street banker Jacob Schiff and his London partner Sir Ernst Cassell, the personal banker to the British Royal Family and to the British Fabian Society. Emma Goldman was a leading member of Britain's Neo-Malthusian League, and when she was expelled from the United States, fellow Neo-Malthusian League member, Lord Bertrand Russell sponsored her safe return to England.

The McKinley assassination was paradigmatic of the British assassination bureau that targeted American presidents and other leading American patriots for execution.

In every instance of such targeting of American leaders, *Executive Intelligence Review* has been able to establish a clear chain-of-command back to London. The only thing that has changed is the incredulousness of the American people, who have tolerated, for too long, the century of assassinations that have robbed the United States and the world of some of its most impassioned and patriotic leaders.

The First Sino-Japanese War, 1894-95 & the Russo-Japanese War, 1904-05

by William Jones

June 5—The tremendous surge of optimism as the Nineteenth Century came to a close, engendered as it was, by the burgeoning Industrial Revolution, and the great scientific discoveries of the previous decades, would come to an abrupt end with the dawning of the Twentieth Century. The First World War would ring its death-knell. After Kaiser Wilhelm II's firing of Bismarck in 1890, and after the 1901 overthrow of the American patriotic faction of the martyred President William McKinley by British Empire stooge Theodore Roosevelt, the stage was set for that first great conflagration of the century.

It had all been designed and choreographed by that evil manipulator, Britain's King Edward VII. While Edward would be long gone before the great destruction of that war began, he had already set the stage in his carefully designed system of alliances, which required only a spark to set off the conflagration. This war would produce a rampant cultural pessimism which still deeply infests the cultural life of the Western world. While what was then called "The Great War," was to be followed by another that was even greater in its extent and in its casualties, the First World War essentially created the disastrous trajectory from which the Western world has never yet been able to free itself.

But the origins of that war were already visible beforehand in events occurring in the Far East. The British Empire still reigned supreme there, although its sea dominance was being called into question by the growing maritime power of the United States. Also in Asia, the 1852-54 opening of Japan by Commodore Matthew Perry, and the "unequal treaties" imposed on China, were impelling these nations to move rapidly onto the road to industrialization, if they were to remain independent. In British India there were also rumblings by patriotic elements eager to overthrow the British yoke.

Faced with the impending curtailment of its global power by all of these new factors, the British Imperial elite was seeking allies in the region on which to pin its hopes. The choice fell on the fellow island nation of Japan. U.S. policy, while often compromised by self-seeking comprador elements eager to make a killing in the Far East, was generally geared to safeguarding and maintaining the independence of the nations there, and, on the basis of trade and economic growth, to preserving mutually beneficial relations with all of its countries.

This policy was underlined by former President Ulysses S. Grant, when he visited these countries during a trip around the world in 1877. In a letter to the State Department from Tokyo on Aug. 13, 1879, Grant wrote:

> In the vast East, embracing more than two-thirds of the human population of the world, there are but two nations even partially free from the domination and dictation of some one or other of the European powers, with intelligence and strength enough to maintain their independence: Japan and China are the two nations. The people of both are brave, intelligent, frugal, and industrious. With a little more advancement in modern civilization, mechanics, engineering, etc., they could throw off the offensive treaties which now cripple and humiliate them, and could enter into competition for world commerce. Much more employment for the people would result from the change, and vastly more effective would it be. They would become much larger consumers as well as producers, and thus the civilized world would be vastly benefited by the change, but none so much as China and Japan.

Grant had also seen on his trip the oppressive nature of the British yoke in India, and was appalled by it.

In his visits to Japan and China, both countries asked Grant to help mediate between them, over their conflicting territorial claims to the Ryukyu Islands—claims eventually resolved in favor of Japan. Chinese Minister Li Hongzhang appealed to Grant to use his prestige to attempt to negotiate a solution to the conflict. Grant agreed to do so, and encouraged the State Department to continue to work to preserve amity between these two nations, noting that if the two parties came to war, the British would subdue them both.

Japan's First War With China

Before long, however, Great Britain was working on Japan to transform it into its "marcher-lord" in the Asia-Pacific region. From 1872 until 1888, the British ran a program to train Japanese naval officers. British naval officers taught at the Tokyo Naval College. From 1870 to 1900, most Japanese battleships were built in British yards. Although the two nations would not sign a formal mutual defense treaty until 1902, their collaboration was already well advanced when Japan became intent on eliminating Chinese dominance in Asia, in order to establish their own control over Korea.

Korea was formally under Chinese suzerainty, but Japan, now building up its military power, had a growing diplomatic presence on the peninsula. Russia also had significant political influence over the Korean king. Both China and Russia were seen by the Japanese as potential competitors in their attempts to dominate Asia. A contrived "uprising" by Korean nationalists led to the pro-Japan faction at the Korean court "requesting" Japanese troops to help suppress the rebellion in 1894, and the movement of Japanese troops to Korea

An October 1905 cartoon of Britain (left) and Japan (right) cementing the Anglo-Japanese alliance. Published in Punch, *a British satirical magazine.*

placed them in direct conflict with China. This, not 1914, was the actual date on which the First World War began.

While China was also attempting to build up its military power and was purchasing warships from abroad under a program laid out by Li Hongzhang, the main diplomat and modernizer at the Qing Court, the training of Chinese sailors lagged behind, and the Japanese scored an easy naval victory over China in this first Sino-Japanese War of 1894-95. Afterwards, the Japanese considered the Liaodong Peninsula in Manchuria to be part of their "war booty." The successful efforts of Russian Finance Minister Sergei Witte to mobilize the other European powers (except for Britain) to prevent Japan from occupying the Liaodong Peninsula, left even greater animosity among the Japanese militarists against Russia. The war did, however, place Korea, Taiwan, and the Pescadores Islands under the Japanese Empire. Japan's quick victory over China also increased its confidence in taking on the more powerful Russia in the Far East.

A Eurasian Land-Bridge

Russia was interested in far more than the Korean situation. Witte was attempting to unite the far-flung Russian Empire by the construction of a railroad through Siberia. For Witte, a student of German economist Friedrich List, the railroad would also provide a corridor of development for Russia, making Russia the prime conduit for the transportation of goods between Asia and Europe, and, as the British were keen to note, the major competitor to the British sea-based trade.

As construction on the railroad was proceeding,

Witte developed the idea of building it to the coast via a shorter route through Chinese Manchuria. This would help to cement Russia's relationship with China, and would serve to make inroads for Russia into the Chinese market as well. Witte negotiated a twenty-year lease with Li Hongzhang to build and operate the railroad during that time, with the intent of then handing it over to China. Aware of the rising tensions with Japan, Witte was also aiming to bring Japan into a commercial relationship whereby it also could ship their goods along the railroad line. Witte wrote:

> It's possible, that thanks to the construction of the Chinese Eastern Railroad, in the near future, we will become closer to Japan because of our trade and industrial interests, and closer relations between countries in that realm seems one of the most powerful factors in the elimination of military conflict between nations.

But in the end, the Japanese drive for hegemony, and the British manipulation of their "marcher-lord" in an effort to undermine Russia, would bring Witte's plans to naught.

Witte's railroad also presented an obstacle to British domination over the Eurasian heartland. Witte had effectively brought together the major land powers of Europe—France, Germany, and Russia—in a de facto alliance for development. The construction of the Trans-Siberian Railroad would serve to unite the rail links from the Atlantic to the Pacific, a land-bridge which would relegate British control of the sea to a subordinate status in world trade. The outlines of the Edwardian policy toward this development were elaborated most succinctly by Halford Mackinder, who warned of loss of British control over the Eurasian landmass, were this railroad to become a reality. Britain was intent on destroying the Witte alliance.

Britain Backs Japan's War vs. Russia

Witte's policy was quickly undermined by British operations in the Far East. In 1902, the British signed a mutual defense treaty with Japan, the Anglo-Japanese Treaty, which assured Japan that Russia would have no allies if Japan were to go to war against it. Secondly, the British had encouraged Kaiser Wilhelm to pressure Tsar Nicholas to move against Japan, by raising the

specter of the "Yellow Peril." In addition, a profitable logging operation on the Yalu River by a Tsarist court cabal, was pushing for the occupation of Manchuria, an action which would effectively torpedo Russia's relations with China and be seen as a direct provocation by Japan—something that Witte strenuously warned against. But Nicholas foolishly went along with the scheme.

In the ensuing Russo-Japanese War of 1904-05, which was considered the first modern war of the Twentieth Century, the Russian Navy was annihilated. While the Russian Army was still intact and fighting, the still-uncompleted railroad made it difficult to maintain its needed logistical support. Anglophile Teddy Roosevelt, who had taken over the White House after the assassination of President McKinley, offered his "services" as a mediator, to bring the two parties to the peace table. While the Japanese were largely victorious, they had suffered heavy losses and were therefore prepared to talk, knowing that the American President was in full sympathy with their demands.

Witte, who was assigned as the Russian representative at the peace talks, was a tough negotiator. Although Russia had to cede the Kurile Islands and half of Sakhalin Island to Japan, Russia avoided paying the heavy indemnity that Japan had demanded. Russia's military defeat, however, had more serious consequences—leading ultimately to the downfall of the Tsar and the Bolshevik Revolution of 1917.

The stage was now set for the main drama to unfold. Japanese ambitions had been whetted by its military successes against China and Russia. Japan was now prepared to strike out in a bid to become the dominant power in the Far East. Manchuria, which Witte had withheld from them, would be the first major territory to fall to the Japanese, providing the springboard for its attack against China in 1938, an attack which was the actual beginning of the Second World War.

In Europe, a Russian Empire sapped by war and revolution (indeed already in its death-throes), would be easily enticed into the British web. Russia concluded a treaty with Great Britain in 1907, which brought Russia and its French allies in a tripartite alliance pitted against Germany. World War I had now been fully prepared; it was just waiting for a spark to set it off. The spark came on June 28, 1914 in Sarajevo, with the assassination of Austrian Archduke Franz Ferdinand.

LAROUCHE FIRESIDE CHAT

We Have Within Us, The Power of Victory

This discussion took place between Lyndon LaRouche and hundreds of political activists from across the United States, in the LaRouchePAC activists' conference call June 4, 2015. John Ascher was the host.

John Ascher: Good evening, everyone. This is John Ascher in Leesburg, Virginia welcoming everyone to the third "Fireside Chat" with Lyndon LaRouche, who is on with us live this evening. I'd like to welcome all of the assembled members and supporters of the La-Rouche movement. If you are on for the first time, I'd like to give you a special welcome.

Lyn, do you want to make any preliminary remarks here this evening?

Lyndon LaRouche: Just one, which is a matter of settling unfinished business. We had a report presented from a member, an associate, of ours, and it was fairly important because it deals with the distinction between the idea of using trains on tracks, which has a certain validity, of course, naturally. But there's a higher level of importance, which I think we may come to discuss in the course of events.

The fact is that the principles of science, physical science, are not based on simple, ordinary kinds of algebra—and algebra doesn't do it. Because the actual nature of mankind is presented by people such as Nicholas of Cusa, such as great scientists, the founder of the understanding of what the Solar System is [Johannes Kepler], and also, more significantly, more recently, the galactic principle—the fact that human life is located *within* the domain of the galactic sphere. That's science. Very few people are aware of it, but that's the fact, and in due course, we can encounter that issue again.

The British Empire vs. the American System

Q: This is R— from Brooklyn. I'd like to say good evening to Mr. LaRouche, and I'd also like to say he talked last week about the fact that the British were responsible for our aggravation. I find that in talking to people, and telling people this, and communicating it, and discussing that, in my opinion, Winston Churchill was not a nice guy, and several other things, I constantly find myself having to do education in terms of the history of this. People don't seem to quite grasp it, and a lot of this, I take it, is because our educational system has been skewed to present anything but! In other words, the British were our good buddies, we fought a war with them, and blah, blah, blah. And that's about how the education system leaves it. As far as I'm concerned, Churchill—ugh! But the average person I talk to doesn't quite grasp it, and it's difficult sometimes to get this over. I wonder if you have any more comment on that.

LaRouche: Well, sure. The fact is that we are victims of a British Empire system. We used to be an American System, but over the course of time, a certain group from the British Empire circles became stronger and stronger. We had major fights to bring certain Presidents into a leading position, and a very few of our Presidents, who were elected as Presidents, were really competent in terms of representing what the principles of our Constitution are.

And this is the reality we have to face.

But the other side of the point is, if we do *not* understand what the American System represents, as in the case of great leaders, such as great creative people in our history, we fail. Because we get sidetracked. We are diverted from our mission, which was given to us. So, that's what our problem is.

Q: This is G— from Los Angeles, and I'm speaking to the nature of the British Empire, and our culture as an extension: that there is a theory—I'm paraphrasing—that we were originally complete beings which featured insight and feats of awareness, and at one point, a force from the Cosmos came in and pressed upon us their mind, their mind being covetousness, greed, cowardice, and above all, fear. That fear, and their fear of exposure, which they gave to us.

And in my lifetime, what I've experienced, is [a shift from] my grandparents and parents, influenced by FDR, with essentially pride and justice, to the culture we have now, which is really endless sources of conflict and fear. I'd just like a comment on that.

LaRouche: Sure. Well, in practice we have a very hot and very particular kind of situation, in terms of the electoral process ongoing at this time. We have [Martin] O'Malley, who is a leading candidate, actually, and we have others in that same category, who are important. Our struggle now is to clean up the issues of the ongoing election campaign; we're already in an ongoing election campaign process. The question is: what are we going to do? What's our policy? What should our policy be? And right now, my view, of course, is that I'm behind what I have been for a long time—in terms of the principles of policy, U.S. policy. I haven't changed much; I've been improved, I should say, more than anything else.

But the point is that I'm now backing, personally, what is represented by O'Malley, and by some other people who go into the same category. Because the other choices I see presented on us, are not something we want to have, if we look at the consequences of what these candidacies mean. So I'm actively involved in that, and I have, of course, a scientific view of how the economy works—I'm a follower of Alexander Hamilton, one of the greatest people, I think, in U.S. history.

These are the people whom I respect the most.

Q: This is C— from Boston. Good evening, Mr. LaRouche, sir. You know, since this week was the press conference to release the 28 pages of the 9/11 report, I was just wondering—you know, I've studied it, I've looked into it for a few years, finding the official story to be a fairy tale, to be honest, from the overwhelming evidence we've received. Would there ever be a time in

Library of Congress

Sir Winston Churchill, with his son Randolph and grandson Winston, dressed for the coronation of Queen Elizabeth II.

the future where the people would be held responsible for that, like indictments?

LaRouche: I think we have to make it that way right now.

Now, you see this case of O'Malley. I cannot give you a final judgment on O'Malley's campaign. I can say that so far, it's the brightest one that I've seen on the horizon. And with good reason. His credentials are excellent. They're limited in some degree, but any Presidential candidate who's coming seriously into the candidacy, is generally an ingénue, relatively speaking.

So, he represents that, and he represents the principles that represents. He has a very significant history, political history, in terms of this, and I think so far, he stands up very well.

Now, I know that's not the last answer on the whole thing. But right now, I would say he's the man on the case. Maybe he won't be that in the end, but right now, he is. His ostensible rivals at this time are not worth supporting.

LPAC/Matthew Ogden

The June 2 press conference featuring Sen. Rand Paul's introduction of a Senate resolution calling for the release of the classified 28 pages of the 9/11 Inquiry Report. Former Senator Bob Graham is at the microphone.

On the Edge of World War III

Q: My name is R—, legally from New York. I'm a 9/11 survivor, and a first-responder before the first responders even got there. I want to say "thank you," Mr. LaRouche. I can't find words to express my gratitude for all of those, including Angela [Vullo], and the rest, being there Tuesday, with regards to the 28 pages.[1]

I was a CFO, COO, transitional CEO, on Wall Street. As I said, I was in 9/11. I was blown back from... [audio loss] 10 times on my head. I was on the South side. I have over 200 pictures I've never released, and I released six of them last year in New York, at the release of a movie that came out then.

I've read your stuff. I've always followed you. We both are in total agreement—or, I'm in agreement with you. You're my senior and my mentor. I agree with *all* your financial stuff. I love the big picture, the world big picture, that benefits the American interests; and look at places such as Russia, who was our greatest ally in the Revolutionary War, and shamefully, American kids don't even know these things, because they're not taught these things, essentially because of the British monarch, who, I don't know how people forget that they're our greatest enemy, and never ceased to be our greatest enemy. Nor have all those affiliated with them, and there's no need for me to go into that just to show that I know it. Like I said, I yield to you.

Again, I want to thank you. Please know that I had dinner with [Sen.] Rand Paul and his wife about a month ago, and just know, that he's the real deal on this issue. That I can tell you.

And as you have written, the BAE report and what have you—the way you were able to line this all up, going back to 1985, with the London oil deal with the Saudis, with 600,000 barrels still being delivered to London to this very day, for the exchange of BAE Systems and defense—which is the British monarch—who actually had places and offices right down in the heart of America's secrecy and military in Pensacola—Eglin Air Force Base; I know you know of these things, because that's where I live now. I couldn't stay in New York, because it just became so hopeless. I've had my spine reconstructed many times—I'll let Angela fill you in on that.

I look very much forward. I just am recovering from another surgery, from injuries from then, but am so much trying to be at your events, and please know I'm there. I can't thank you enough. If there's anything I can do, anytime you want me to speak, whatever—I'm there for you. Again, I can't thank you—we do have to educate, not only our young, but those who were put through the ROTC system, and the JAGs, especially, in the military, in the '70s and '80s, because they can't grasp what Andrew Jackson made obvious. I mean, these people burned down our White House in 1812! Did the Russians do that? I don't recall them doing any-

---

1. See "<u>Bill</u> To Declassify 28 Pages Now in the U.S. Senate."

NATO

Barack Obama meets with NATO Secretary General Jens Stoltenberg on May 26, 2015.

thing like that. But I'm just trying to point out some things, and I think you understand.

My question is this: They really are coming at us with everything they have right now. As I said, I lived in 9/11. After I got blown back, I was back in those Towers. My fiancée was in there—she never came out. She was where the plane went in, the second plane. And I know exactly what went down. There's no mistake. The official story is, as the last caller said, an absolute fairy tale, *absolute* fairy tale.

But what is more important, is what I heard earlier: We need to understand that not only did the U.S. Patriot Act come about because of it, but there was something much bigger, which you speak to, which has to do with the British monarch, which enabled them to push us into the financial repression beginning in 2009, with that crash, and with the derivatives of over $600 billion—all of this bringing everything into the three to five regions that they intend to do, to control manufacturing and production in the globe, using things like Agenda 21 and things of that nature.

They are moving now. There is no turning around, and I know you know this, because you say it. And I do see it. And I firmly, firmly believe that we are right

around the corner from another 9/11 attack—which is going to be much worse. It won't just be anthrax this time—as you know, it was reported yesterday—sent to 17 different states and Washington, D.C. Now, why would that be happening?

LaRouche: We're on the edge of a world war. A world war like nothing we've experienced before. If this occurs, if the United States, under Obama, does what Obama indicates he's going to do, the chances of survival of the human species are pretty dim.

Now, obviously, the condition is to get Obama out of power over the United States government. But it's actually power run by the British interest, the British Empire. And our problem is, to stop this war, which would be an extermination war, if it actually happens—to prevent that war from occurring.

Now that doesn't mean we're going to go with humility—it means we're going to go with good discretion. And it has to be done.

At the same time, we see that over the course of the Twentieth Century, the United States has actually been in a long wave of decline in terms of the conditions of life, which we supplied to our own citizens; the conditions of life in general; the chances for the future. We see what happens to our children, or young people generally; of the degeneration of their ability to cope with reality.

So, we have a mission orientation. It's not only from the United States. We also have to deal with the fact that we have nations, in parts of Asia, in South America, and in Europe and elsewhere; that we have a responsibility, through the responsibilities of the United States itself, as a nation. We must achieve a guarantee that a thermonuclear war will not occur. Because if a thermonuclear war occurs, between the ostensible powers in conflict today, that could be—probably—an extermination of the human species.

That's where we are.

Now what that means is, if you don't dump Obama out of the Presidency, and you allow him to run out the end of his term, he's getting very close to pushing the United States into a thermonuclear war, from which the United States itself would not recover. And he's a British agent anyway—it's well-known. But the problem is, we stuck him in there. It should never have happened. It wouldn't have happened if the Bush family hadn't been in there. It was the Bush family's intrusion into the election process, which caused the degeneration which led to all these effects, since the early part of the Twentieth Century.

But that's the situation. So, we do have to mobilize.

We do have also responsibility for developing an economic recovery, which assures a reasonable improvement in the life of people in general. Our job as human beings is not to be a success only in our own life. Our purpose in life is, we know we're going to die sooner or later, all of us—each of us is going to die sooner or later. But what we have to do, is consider what we leave behind us for future generations. And that intention, which is the intention for which any soldier of the United States risks his life, in trying to deal with this issue—they risk their lives for the sake of the future of our people, of our nation, and of the world.

And we need that kind of orientation, and we need it urgently now.

State of the U.S. economy: The scene of the May 12 Amtrak train derailment.

Move Obama Out of the Presidency

Q: A— in Orange County, California. I'm wondering if Mr. LaRouche can tell us what we can do to make the people here, the voters, conducive to the candidacy of Martin O'Malley?

LaRouche: There's a lot we can do. That is, each of us can, those of us who know how to deal with these kinds of problems, in particular, we know *exactly* what we have to do. We may not define details, but we know in principle. We know, for example, that we must remove Obama from the Presidency—because Obama's on a course of policymaking, which is aiming directly at World War III. That's what's happening.

Look at what Obama's doing with China. Look at what he's doing otherwise. Look what he's done in Northern Africa. Look at what he's done in many cases. Look at what he's done to the American people. Look at what he's done to the health care for the American citizens, and so forth and so on.

This guy should never have been President. He's a disaster. And we've got to have him ushered out of office.

Now, that doesn't mean we just want *anybody* to replace him. Or our best option may be almost anyone, to get him out of there. But the point is, we need to com-

pose a Presidential campaign, for a Presidential body, which is not just a President, but which is a number of people who have the combined skills, and the abilities otherwise, to make, create a Presidency which will meet the standard which we have not had often, since the Kennedys were killed.

So, this is our situation. We have to pull our citizens to come to understand, that we must move Obama out of the Presidency before he gets that extra margin, which enables him to launch World War III. And I mean, World War III. And with World War III, as launched by Obama, as the trend shows today, there are very few survivors, if any, from the kind of war that Obama is pulling the United States into.

Q: This is F— from Louisiana. Lyn, will you dialogue these effects of regulating the value of money, and of foreign coin, and fixing the standard of weights and measures in the physical economy, which is Article 1 in our Constitution? Will you reflect on that?

The Constitution calls for regulating the value of money, and of foreign coin, and fixing the standard of weights and measures—Article 1 of the Constitution. Lyn, can you discuss that and brief us on how you get the physical economy in balance?

LaRouche: That idea, that concept, that conception is a valid one, but underneath it, there's a more important one. I mean, that's a good example—that's a good starting point for the discussion of that issue. But you have to go to something deeper.

For example, the key thing here is how can we in the United States take this mess we have now—and it is a mess; it's a terrible situation—the situation of the Americans since the Bush Presidency, and now the Obama Presidency, which is much worse. It's destroying the United States, and destroying the rights and so forth of the people. So, we have to get that cleaned up.

The first question is: Throw Obama out of office. Because if you don't throw him out of office, you're not going to get anywhere. He's on the road to launching, or provoking the launching, of thermonuclear war, globally, and that would be pretty much the extermination of the human species.

So, the other thing is, what are we going to do, presuming that we keep Obama from destroying the world—what are we going to do to deal with the problems we already have here? The problems of economy, the problems of social care, problems of morality, and so forth. So we have a two-fold problem. We have to deal with a threat, which threatens the extinction of our existence, and at the same time, we have to deal with the problems of ending the injustices which were imposed upon our people.

I know that the solutions for these kinds of problems exist. I know what they are. I've had a lot of history in this thing. I know what it is—we can do it. The question is: Can we muster among our people, among our citizens, can we succeed in mustering a sufficient part of our citizens right now, in order to bring about a forced action, primed by the desire of our citizens, to say "We are not going to war. We are getting tired of this starvation. We don't want to be cheated any more. We don't want the people who have been cheating us to have any more control over us."

That's about the short of it. And that's a good place—if you want to get a bigger discussion of the thing, that's a good place to start.

Q: This is B— with the New York group. I'm a World War II veteran, Mr. LaRouche, and I've got you by a little bit, because I'm 95 years of age. I went over in the third wave of invasion in Europe, and when things kind of quieted down a little bit, I had a one-on-one with General de Gaulle. But what's troubling me now as the tickler, is the people who are poisoning our food. Are you aware of this, and do you have any particular means at your disposal to offset the poisoning of our food?

I'm listening.

LaRouche: Okay. Of course I know about that. There are all kinds of aspects to it. The very fact that we are cheated in our food; the fact we're being deprived of access to nourishment that we need. That's all there. But what we're seeing now is a product of a process that's been going on for a great deal of time.

I, as you did, belonged to the period of World War II. You were obviously serving in World War II, as part of it. We were also serving in the intermediate periods, we were trying to fight against those people who were destroying the rights of our citizens, even then. And in the face of the fact that we had Presidents who got assassinated, and not much was done about that, in curing that problem. We've come to the point that we must be determined, as a group of people, we must be determined to ensure—at your age, of course, it's more important than ever—to be assured that we have secured the kind of situation, the kind of society, which we require for the future of coming generations of our citizens.

Because we're all going to die. The point is, the meaning of life is not dying. The meaning of life is what you can accomplish for the future while you're still alive. And that's my principle. You're a little older than I am, by a significant stretch. But that's where it is.

Water and the Galaxy

Q: This is K— from Silicon Valley in California. Mr. LaRouche, again, thank you for being on the call tonight. It is a real honor to get to speak to you.

I'm asked to help out with donations periodically for the LaRouchePAC and that takes money. My concern is that it seems like money, unfortunately, drives our system entirely. And it discourages me to see our mass media join in with so many who want to demonize China and Russia, and as you said, lead us toward war. What's an effective way to battle that monetarism that just runs the world?

LaRouche: Well, the problem is—take the case of California. Now some time ago, we had a governor in California [Edmund G. "Pat" Brown, 1959-67] who was a very good governor. But that was some time back, before other people got in there, including the current governor [Jerry Brown]. What they're doing now, is they're proposing that we have to draw down the access to water, which is the water of life, really. And they're saying we have to withdraw that water from the citizens not only of California, but of the states that are in the overall area. So, we're in a struggle right now, a strug-

USDA/David Kosling

A dried-up former riverbed along Highway 99 near Bakersfield, California—in February 2014.

gle to prevent a systematic mass killing of the citizens of the United States, in particular. That's what's behind what the present governor of California has done publicly. That's why he's opposed publicly.

So therefore, these are the kinds of things that make many people think that maybe there's something *wrong* in the political process now, inside the United States, not just in California.

Well, there is no reason, no scientific reason, why we have to dry up the resources of water in California. Because there are difficulties, which have to be overcome to deal with the water problem in California. They are serious ones. But there are scientific principles which we could put to work, and develop to put to work, which can address this issue.

The control of water—just to get to the fact of the matter—the control is not based on water on Earth. Yes, water on Earth is a very significant part, of the water available to mankind. *But* the source of the security of water by humanity, is not located on Earth; it's located in the galaxy. That is, the galactic process is a source. All the problems that we have dealing with the water problem such as in California—how do we use our technology, our skills and technology, to manage some of that water, which is circling around us, and is involved in that area? How do we get into moving it into areas where the water that we need on Earth is actually prompted to come down?

If we address that problem, which is a problem which does lend itself to solutions—if we do that, it requires a higher level of technology—but we can do it. The galactic system is also reflected by the system of Earth anyway. So, that's where we are.

We are threatened from our own government, inside the United States, at present, which is depriving our citizens of the means of having sufficient water to maintain the existing population of our nation. And we should take that exemplary case, and let that be the root of our motivation, to fix some of the things that need to be fixed.

Shut Down Wall Street

Q: This is E— in Los Angeles. Mr. LaRouche, it is an honor and a privilege to be talking with you this evening. Two weeks ago, a lady called in and asked you about ISIS and how to defeat it militarily, and you referenced her to the Congress, which, of course, there's no doubt there; they're all ready to send weapons to these terrorists. But isn't ISIS actually, in fact, a front for the Western oligarchy, as we've seen in Libya, and are, as a matter of fact, currently seeing in Syria? So, ultimately, even a creation of British-America and British-Arabia, and even the 51st state of Israel, to squelch resistance in the Middle East, and put them under the boot of the Empire?

LaRouche: I would say that Israel is not the major problem. You've got some bad choices of leaders in Israel, but if you understand the history of Israel, in its modern game, you understand some of these things, and you find that most of the Israeli population is not evil, though some people in that orbit may be evil in terms of the consequences of what they do.

But that's not the issue. The issue is simply: The British Empire, the British Royal Empire, which is the Mother of the Saudi Kingdom, and related things. These terrible things, including the role of the British royal family—which is an evil force—these are the things we have to free mankind from. And if we get rid of the various crooks in our own nest, and deal with the problem of the British Empire and deal with some other things of that nature, we find that the world at large, in terms of the general population of the planet, is trying to move in a direction which is nobler than anything we've experienced for a long period of time.

You look at what's happened in China. You look at what's happening in India right now. You look at what's happening in certain other parts of the world. And you see that the nations are struggling to bring themselves into a state of betterment, of self-government and government in general, which is good. It may not be perfect, but it's good, and it's going in the right direction.

Actually, the greatest part of the population of the planet, is actually pushing for a good situation of relations among states and peoples. So that's there.

Our problem is: We, in the United States, as well as what we have to do with the nations of Europe and so forth—what we have to do is we have to get rid of Wall Street. That's the first thing we have to do. Don't you know that? Look, Wall Street is bankrupt, totally bankrupt. But nobody will let it get shut down, because it's protected by the Wall Street interests.

Now, if we would shut down Wall Street, because it is a fraud, because it *is* worthless, we would find—and if we turned our policies back to what they were, say, 50 years ago, we would very rapidly move in a positive direction, for life in general, and for conditions of life.

So, I think that's the way you have to look at it. On the one hand we know that the evil is there, the problem is there. But we also know the majority of the planet, in terms of national forces, is actually aiming for common good things to happen. They may not always agree with each other, but they are trying to move in that direction. And what we want to do is get the United States free of Obama, and free of what he represents—the Bushes, for example. Get rid of that. And by that means, we can turn the United States population into an effective force to free us from the problems that curse us from within at this time.

We Don't Have a Jewish Problem

Q: My name is D—. I'm in Indianapolis. What I wanted to ask you about is Israel. As I see it, you give Israel a break that you do not give to the Saudis. You've been asking for the 28 pages, and I'm behind you on that. But I think you had the dancing Israelis, you had the dual citizenship Israeli-Americans in Congress, and the Administration. I think that you've given Israel a break, and not attributed their responsibility to what's happening in the world today.

LaRouche: There's a fact here, and I know the fact very well, because, you know, I've been around all over

creative commons
The New York Stock Exchange on Wall Street, New York City.

the world, back and forth, a few times around. And I also know what goes on in our country.

I also understand the whole anti-Semitic stuff in the United States. I've lived since a youth with that issue. And people would say I was Jewish. Well, I'm not Jewish, but they thought I was, because I wasn't on this other side.

But you know, we don't have a Jewish problem, not really. That doesn't exist. You may have isolated cases, people who are gangster-inclined, and so forth, but that's not the general thing. The Jewish population is actually very close to what's called the Christian population. There's not that much difference. There's difference in terms of bad face, bad things, bad behavior, but in general, in the history of Jewry in the United States, and in parts of Europe, plus the Hitler nonsense, and also some French nonsense, and some Italian nonsense—the French nonsense, in particular.

But there was no problem like that, no systemic problem. There are special conditions which are induced by pressures of various kinds, and they produce hateful attitudes of those who feel they're victimized and those who feel they want to victimize somebody else. So, it's not really that kind of a problem.

If we have a United States which is functioning as it should, without Wall Street—eliminate Wall Street! That's the key to a lot or problems. And again, you talk about normal people, normal people with Jewish religious backgrounds and so forth—you don't really have much of a problem. No more problem than with any next-door neighbor you have.

So, the very idea that we have to have an anti-Semitic, or a counter-anti-Semitic thing, is not really a legitimate issue. Because the issue is something which reflects a *part* of what should not have occurred, which did occur. And that's the way to look at it. But there's no reason to say there's any systemic, justified conflict between Jews and Christians, for example.

Ascher: I say "Mazel tov" to that, Lyn. So, here's the next person up.

Russian Ministry of Defense/Antov Blinov

One of the many Russian surprise combat exercises held recently. This one was in the Kaliningrad region March 20, 2015.

The Common Interests of Nations

Q: This is B— from Washington. Where do I start? Well, I signed the BRICS petition, and if everybody did that, that might change Wall Street, right? Yeah, and I'm going to go get some cattle prods and hand them out down there in Washington, D.C., and get the Congress people to get off their ass, and stand up and impeach Obama. That's all I've got to say.

LaRouche: Let me say one thing in response to that. We have two cases now of people who, along with O'Malley, are ready to move, to create an election process for the United States, to create a new composition of our center of government, and if we do that, and get away without thermonuclear war in the meantime, I think that we have entered a new period.

For example, let's look at South America, or most of South America. What I know is going on in South America is a very beautiful change for the better. Similarly, we see what's happening in China. What's happening in China is essentially, from the standpoint of statecraft, beautiful. What's happening in Russia is actually quite beautiful. And Russia has a legacy of capability, in engineering, science, and so forth, which is very important. You have also, in other parts of Europe, where they have bad conditions now, those conditions can be cured.

Remember: Spain, Portugal, France also, and especially Italy, have been abused. They've been suppressed. They've been reduced to poverty, to a great degree, and a very serious degree of repression. And therefore, all we have to do is change our attitude sometimes, and recognize that what's going on is, bad conditions globally, and not those conditions which are desired by the populations more generally. And we have to operate from that standpoint.

We've got to a point now, where we cannot fight general warfare any more. General warfare in its present stage of technology would be the extermination of the human species. What we're confronted with at this time, is that if Obama is not removed from the Presidency, if he's not kicked out of office, the danger is that he is moving rapidly for causing a global thermonuclear war, a war which could lead, probably, to the extermination of the human species.

So our objective is not to say, how can we win wars? Any competent general officer in the United States, and in similar nations, knows that. So why are we toying with this junk? Why are we playing this game? Because of a few Nazis, like those in Ukraine? They're really not most of the Ukrainian people, but most of the Ukrainian people are under the control of a Nazi party inside Ukraine.

So, if we deal with these problems, and threats of warfare, and get nations to recognize what the greatest injustices are that are going on right now, we have a reason to bring nations to recognize that they have a *common* interest. They may have different ways of functioning, somewhat different objectives. But we know that the interest of those nations, those peoples—their interest is to benefit from the kinds of options which should be made available to them right now. And that's us too. So, it's in our common interest, to share our common interest with some other people in other nations.

Q: I want to ask Mr. LaRouche a question: How can we do this? You need the political party to listen to the voters. They seem to have a mind of their own, and we understand that they actually have a different agenda. How can we get Mr. Obama out of office, or do we have to wait until his term ends?

LaRouche: No, you don't! The way his term ends—because his end will be your end, and you don't want that!

No, we've got to get this guy out of there, and it can be done. The O'Malley campaign for President, right now, which is coming into focus, with some other things which are related to that, there is a movement of resistance against what Obama represents, and what some of the worst Republicans represent; also at the same time, the opportunists, that sort of thing. So we have the reason to wish and to act to free ourselves of these diseases: We must do it! We *can* do it! We simply have to put our minds to it, and we'll find we can do it. I *know* we can do it: I get a good smell, for this kind of thing.

The Right To Be Free of Tyranny

Q: This is B— in L.A. My question for LaRouche—and how are you, sir?

LaRouche: I'm old and happy.

Q: My question would be that the situation seems to be generating in people a quality of retreat, and you stated lately about this—how do we snap people out of this? Obviously, the conditions by which we are getting people out of this, would be to take on the beauty inside people's souls in order for them to see what has to be done, in order to get rid of this evil. So my question to you is, under these conditions, what would be the conditions by which humanity will actually save themselves away from this existential threat?

LaRouche: What do you think, for example, that the typical person, often deprived, especially broadly, nationally here—deprived, intimidated, beaten, so forth, demoralized, what do you think that that all-so-typical citizen throughout our United States—don't you think those citizens would like to be free? Would like to escape from the kind of tyranny which Wall Street, for example, represents? Why do you think so many people in the United States are poor? Because Wall Street does it! Wall Street has gained the power to come in and rob you, and rob the nation generally, of everything.

If you look at what happened over the course of the Twentieth Century, into the present period now, here, you see the people of the United States have actually

Xinhua

The starting point of the middle route of China's South-North Water Diversion Project, one of the beautiful projects transforming that nation.

been deprived, increasingly, as a whole, over the entire period since the Twentieth Century began. Don't you think that those Americans, if they're not tortured into some kind of obscenity, would like to have a decent life? Don't you think that parents would wish they could have decent children, who can live and be successful? Don't you think that people with hunger, who are being robbed and suppressed, would not like to be freed of that?

The problem is, we who have the spark and experience, must encourage our fellow citizens to join together with us, to bring about the action, the political action which throws the tyrants out of their pews!

Q: This is K— in Moline, Illinois. President Obama's mother and maternal grandparents worked for the CIA, and that's been covered up because they don't want the people to know that he has any connection like that to the CIA.

LaRouche: We're aware that there's a certain truth to that. When you look at it on the facts of the case, as presented normally, that's a very simple way of look at what the abuse is that people are suffering, actually suffering.

The problem is, we have to look at the other side. We have to concentrate on what the measures are which are available to our hand, to change that. It's when people submit to oppression, that oppression takes over a nation, and if you don't have a certain kind of insolence, about people being pushed around, then you give in, you give in to tyranny. And I've been a stubborn cuss, and I can say, fairly without any exaggeration, that I've always been on that side, the side that the people in general have a right to be independent of tyranny.

But I would say also, that the tyranny applied to our people, in terms of bad education, bad job opportunities, everything you want to talk about, every kind of deterioration and fraud that's been happening to our people, *we let it happen*. And I think the time has come—I've been at this a long time—I've been fighting this fight for a long time, but we're on the edge of an option of winning. And the time to *win*, to muster ourselves, and to go out into the election campaign theater, and get a new President in place, now, *I think we can do it!* Because Wall Street is *bankrupt*. Wall Street is bankrupt: It has no value.

Take the case of what's going on in Europe. Throughout Europe, generally: Europe is bankrupt! The British Empire is bankrupt! That is, all the swindlers are implicitly, thus bankrupt.

But, on the other hand, there are technologies which exist, which are available—you've seen what's happening in China, what's happening in India, despite the problems they have now with the weather system; but we're seeing in South America, we're seeing elsewhere. We see that in the world, there is a virtual majority of the population of the planet, they're ready! They're oriented in that direction! All we have to do, is join with them, around the same issue. We must create a better world for the human beings who inhabit it. That's the simple version of what we must do. The time has come to do it.

Now, I think on the case of O'Malley and what is associated with him,—I think there's a potential coming out, right now, at us, in which we have reached the point, which O'Malley expresses, and he expresses it adequately, because he has a history which fits this story: That if we move, now, on the basis of saying we're going to get a better system of government, that is a new institution of government, which is better than this crap we've been subjected to for the past eight years; and if we do that, we are on the road to a new, and better world, than we have known in a very long time.

The True Purpose of Human Life

Q: Hello this is W— in Virginia. You know, all these people still wondering what ISIS is, and this is just short comment before my question. But you might have them understand who ISIS is, if they understood what the dynamics behind the Confederacy were.

My question is around the continuing development—the genesis of the effort to get the release of the 28 pages, which actually goes back to when Mr. La-Rouche was on a talk radio show the day that the 9/11 attacks occurred, when he exposed the cause of what was really behind the attacks. And I was just wondering if he could comment on the relevancy of the most recent press conference to release the 28 pages—if that really reflects a more developed understanding as to what's really behind this, and how it can actually accomplish getting Obama out of office?

LaRouche: I can use a military example. From my observation of warfare, and what its effects are—that there are two things that you can do when you're going to war: One is to run away, and the other is to charge ahead! But don't charge foolishly, but rather deploy yourself with such a force that you actually have a chance at victory!

But victory lies in the attitude largely of the soldier, and those around them; the courage to realize what the thing is that should be done, that must be done, and that it can be done. And that's where we are now. We're at that point: Can we as citizens of the United States, in this United States, these citizens here, can they capture a memory of the courage of the United States in fighting deadly wars, such as World War I and World War II? Can we cope with that? Can we cope with that effort? Can we act accordingly? Can we lay down our lives at risk in order to ensure that the future of mankind, of our people, will be secured, and better, because we took the chance to win that battle? That's the question.

To me, it's a rather obvious one, because I have an attitude about life and death. I'm not a person who wants to die. I'm just willing to think much about it. I had a few occasions to think something about that; but it was never really a big thing for me. My concern was the shame of not doing the thing that you knew you had to do. That's still my policy. I will not give in, to betray, what I know my responsibility is. And, if we get more people doing that, and who can be encouraged to do that—we have within us, the *power* of victory.

Q: First of all, it's an honor to be speaking with you gentlemen. My name is J—, and I'm a U.S. soldier, and resident of California. My question is, how can I support and educate others in my job field, about the goals of the LaRouchePAC, without opposing my boss, the President? And, how can I show people that are rather ignorant, that this is actually *for* America, not against America? And that things like the BRICS nations can be an absolute economic blessing to us, if we let it be?

LaRouche: Now, look, we are individuals. We have, particularly in the United States, those of us who

Ken Thomas

The Tomb of the Unknown Revolutionary Soldier in Washington Square, Philadelphia, featuring a replica of Jean-Antoine Houdon's famous sculpture of President Washington.

future of our human species. We live, in order to hope that we've achieved a better future for our successors, than we had for ourselves. And, that's our mission in life. There's no room for cowardice in human life, but to live in such a way that whatever happens to you, or people like you, *that thing must come out, as a plus for the next generation.*

A Better Future for Those Who Follow

Q: This is K—from Massachusetts. You just asked a question, Mr. LaRouche: "Can we make a better future for the next generations?" It's not a case of "can we?" It's a case of "*we have to.*" We *must do it. We must fight to make the future better for the next generations.*

have some decent kind of education, especially some knowledge of some history of our nation, and therefore, we're not fools who have to sit there and be "impressed" by a tyranny or tyrannical attitudes. We don't have to! Sometimes, you get yourself nearly killed, or even actually killed, because you're resisting evil.

But what's the point? The point is: The purpose of human life, the true purpose of a human life, is, don't waste your existence. Which means, if you're putting your life in danger, because you think you have to, for the sake of mankind, you will try to minimize the danger, but you won't back off. You may go sideways, and try to outflank the guy who's out to kill you, but you don't give in like a coward. You don't cringe and collapse!

Because human life is not a permanent thing. Everyone, who, so far as we know—we've heard about Methuselah, but I haven't got the score there; I don't know if those dates are actually true! But the point is, mankind dies; dies within their generation. And yet, they have done great things, in effect, for the next generations; many of them have! So, what's wrong with death, if it comes honorably?

Don't take your own life. Suicide is not an option! There may be a case, where it's an option, but generally suicide is not an option. Cowardice is not an option. Mankind must do the best they can, each, to realize the meaning of the future of humanity. We live, for the

next generations.

LaRouche: Absolutely! Absolutely! The question is, how do we do that? That's the issue: How do we do it?

Well, first of all, look at what we've got. I like to pick on this thing, because I know about it, and we've been doing it, in my group of people, who are working on this thing. We have focused on the fact that the source of water, the supply of water, for the needs of mankind, is not located primarily on Earth. It's located in the galaxy. Now, the challenge, in that respect, is that, how do we manage and control the galaxy? Or, induce the galaxy to help us, in supplying what we need, for example, as water. And, there are techniques which can be applied to induce that effect. Those techniques are known in some degree, but they're not fully enriched. That is, they're not fully understood. But we know it's true.

The greatest source of water for man's requirements, is located in the galaxy, *not on Earth.* There's a large amount of water on Earth, but that amount of water, is not necessarily adequate, to meet the requirements of mankind's residence on Earth. However, we have access to scientific understandings, which will enable us to understand *how* we can improve our access to the use of water, for man's purposes.

Q: I believe in your mission, to make a better future, for those who follow us. But I believe that to do this, we

"But, above all, we concentrate on the children. We have to care for our children."—Lyndon LaRouche. Here, a performance by the Boston Children's Chorus at a local library.

need to know, love, and serve, our Creator, who is God. Then He will help us in our goals to be achieved that you have been discussing.

Currently, America has turned against God, as exemplified by legalized abortion, where we have killed more than a 100 million unborn children, and now, it's gotten to where we may have legalized same-sex marriage. And I think you all know what happened to those, in the Old Testament, in Sodom and Gomorrah. It was totally destroyed.

Okay, so, we now have Obama. It's a possibility that he is being used by God, as a punishment to us.

LaRouche: I don't think God does that. That's not the way it works. What works is the fact that mankind becomes an agent of Satan; that's a better way of putting it, and we don't want people to become Satanic. Because, when you're talking about these kinds of things, you're really talking about things that border on the Satanic: I mean, abuse of people, unjust imprisonment, all these kinds of things. These are *wrongs*. They're wrongs against humanity. And when humanity does those wrongs, then humanity is guilty of a crime. And that's the way to look at it.

The best way we always try to deal with things, should be that we try to induce our fellow human beings, to abandon things that are inherently destructive. And that's as far as we really want to go. If we find the person who is a criminal, who can't be controlled, who's going to kill people, or do other serious damages, well, it's per-

fectly lawful to put them under restraint. Not to abuse them, but to put them under restraint. Try to induce them to change their ways. That's real.

And the best thing is, you know, if you're clever enough, you often can induce people, who would otherwise tend to become criminals, by simply discouraging them from criminality, because you provide them an idea, an image, of what they're doing as being evil. And the fact that they recognize that as being evil, or something equivalent to evil, can be an inducement to people, to get rid of their dirty habits. And we try and do that as much as possible.

But, above all, we concentrate on the children. We have to care for our children. We have to ensure that they're guided safely, before they reach the age of judgment. And that's the important thing. We have to force that through, in the sense of encouraging it. We have to educate students, children. We have to educate them. If they're educated to understand what the world is made of, they won't be stupid. But if we don't educate them, they're likely to become stupid. If they become stupid, they may become criminal.

So, it's in that nature. We, as society, are responsible, to do everything we can, to ensure that our people do not become criminals. That our people, not only do not become criminals, but they realize something good in themselves, which can be brought out in them, with some help.

A New Presidency

Q: This is F— calling from East Orange, New Jersey. How are you, Mr. LaRouche? I met you a couple of years ago.

What I'm wondering—you may have partially answered my question, regarding education of youth, because I'm sure you've seen, down in Newark, the children in the high school have walked out, because they feel as if—because the state of New Jersey is monitoring the educational system. And in Newark and a good many urban areas here in New Jersey, the children are dissatisfied with the type of education that they're getting.

And, my question is, how do we get a handle on that, where we can see that the educational system throughout the country is improved? Where children feel that they are not being neglected? And then also, to stem this gang warfare that we see going on with children. And to prevent another Ferguson, and another Baltimore? Thank you.

LaRouche: All right. Well, let's say that we have O'Malley becoming President, or in the process of becoming President. Now, what would that mean? That would mean that the school system, which has become a travesty, an abomination—this has been going on for a very significant time, two generations, and actually more. It was going bad even during the time I was a student in school. It was bad then. But that was "sweet times" compared to what we've been getting in the past couple of generations; or as we call them, *de*-generations.

And therefore, what's happened to students; what's happened to the school system; what's happened to "culture in the street," is a destruction of the very souls of the human individuals, the young ones. And that means degeneration of the older ones, as a result.

Therefore, if we're going to have a new President—a new Presidency—under a competent President, as opposed to the—you know what I mean, the kind of people I mean: the Bush people. If we're going to do that, then we're going to reverse the trend toward degeneration in the members of our children and adolescents, and so forth. We are going to change the way in which people are employed, something more fitting for human beings.

And I think that, you know, O'Malley, by virtue of, as much as I know about him, would be the kind of President you might want to have, for those reasons.

Ascher: Well, Lyn, I think we're getting right up to the point we had discussed; we've covered tremendous amount of ground here, this evening. You want to give a summary, or shall we take another call?

LaRouche: Well, take another call, and see what happens.

Q: Hi, this is B——. I'm from Houston currently, but I met Lyndon back in 1975-1976. And I like to hear Lyndon on these calls; it's *great!* Direct from the horse's mouth!

I just wanted to say, I got an e-mail today from [Rep.] Beto O'Rourke, in response to a query that I sent

EIRNS

Martin O'Malley at his May 30 announcement of his candidacy for the Democratic Party nomination for President.

to him about H.Res.14, and he said he read the 28 pages, and he's going to co-sponsor H.Res.14. So! He's the Congressman from El Paso.

LaRouche: That's great. Good effort.

Ascher: Lyn, we're at an hour and a half, I think would an appropriate time to get a summary from you, so people can get some more sense of where we should go between here and our next call.

LaRouche: Well, I think the O'Malley case—I'm not going to say conclusively that O'Malley is the solution. What I say is that what I'm looking at, in him, is a very credible case for a good choice, as President. I don't know the last answer. But I know that right now, that among all the options I see out there, in the election process, that he is probably the man we want.

But I would also say, as I've said before on earlier occasions, the important thing here, is not just *a* President. The important thing here is to assemble a group of leaders in the Presidency, as the Presidency system. And we have to get a composition of members of that team, which by its very nature is the kind of agency which should be responsible for the agency of our government at this time. That's what's important.

And I think O'Malley, so far, you can say faithfully, that compared with the, shall we say, not so good people, who are also running for President, that he stands out as being a favorable choice. But to meet that requirement, we're going to have to see in him, a justified assessment of a man qualified to move into the actual procedure of becoming President.

The Promethean Challenge: BRICS, a New Era for Mankind

by Helga Zepp-LaRouche

Schiller Institute

Helga Zepp-LaRouche at the Schiller Institute's June 6 "Decision Day" conference in Manhattan.

Helga Zepp-LaRouche delivered the keynote address to the Schiller Institute's June 6 conference in Manhattan, titled, "Decision Day for Humanity: The U.S. Must Return to Its Founding Principles and Join the BRICS Alliance Now."

Dear friends, I'm very happy to speak to you today on this particular day, which is D-Day, and that should fill us all with the hope that the danger of a new fascism, which is arising in the world, can be defeated—but hopefully with fewer casualties.

I'm saying this because we are right now on the edge of World War III, and we are at that moment, exactly for the same reasons, that caused World War I and World War II: geopolitical interests of an imperial force against the well-being and common good of nations. Because, contrary to myth, world wars do not happen because of conflicts among nations, but because of imperial designs for the benefit of a small oligarchy. That is exactly what is happening right now.

I think anybody who follows even the public domain of news, of TV, or media in general, has plenty of evidence that we are heading toward a strategic confrontation between the United States and NATO, on the one side, and Russia and China on the other. And this is not something planned for the distant future. This is on the table right now. It's planned for this Summer.

Last week, in the Australian media, there was an e-mail published by military analyst John Shindler, who said that he just received an e-mail from an official from NATO, a non-American, who said, "War is on for this Summer—let's hope it will not be nuclear."

Now, if you look at the different flashpoints where this war could erupt, you have the escalation of the Ukraine crisis. Massive fighting escalated this past Wednesday. President Poroshenko claims that Ukraine is already at war with Russia, and he claims that there is a full invasion by Russian forces in eastern Ukraine. This is completely denied by the Russian side. Russian Foreign Minister Lavrov just said, "No. Russia is putting its utmost priority to make sure the Minsk II process is succeeding."

The Ukrainian parliament just made amendments which allow for the admission of armed forces of other states to fight on the territory of Ukraine. So, while it is not excluded that some individual Russians are on the side of eastern Ukraine, the official Russian Army is not, but you have now special troops, mostly from mercenary armies and private institutions of various countries. This bill, by the way, was introduced into the Ukrainian parliament by Prime Minister "Yats," and if you remember, Yatsenyuk is the darling of [Assistant Secretary of State] Victoria Nuland, who imposed him in a coup on the 21st of February 2014.

Now the U.S. Defense Secretary Ash Carter was meeting yesterday in Stuttgart at the U.S.-European Command, with top American defense officials and diplomats to map out a "counter-strategy" to the Russian military operations in Ukraine, and to "reassure our allies." That is always the phrase used to cover for an escalation. And behind closed doors, two dozen generals, ambassadors, and others were discussing whether to expand military exercises, or beef up the assistance to the Baltics or other countries, and who knows what else they were discussing. It was kind of an emergency meeting.

Ash Carter also said that he is very open to the idea of providing Ukraine with lethal weapons. Now that is completely opposed by most of the European countries, especially Germany, France, and others, because it's the opinion of Hollande, Merkel, and others, that if you provide lethal weapons to Ukraine, a country which is utterly bankrupt—the economy is totally collapsed, the population is suffering a humanitarian catastrophe—it will just lead to more killing, and the danger of an escalation. And that's why the Europeans, that's why Merkel, went to Moscow; that's why you have the so-called Minsk group which is trying to solve this problem by peaceful means.

Multiple Military Maneuvers

Why am I saying that the danger is so immediately acute? Well, if you look at the official NATO website, it has an eight-page document there which goes through the different military maneuvers taking place between April and November, and there are major force exercise, but mostly on the Russian periphery, along the Russian borders. Many of those maneuvers are related to the Very High Readiness Joint Task Force, or Spear-

NATO

Scores of ships and aircraft from 17 countries are taking part in these Baltic Sea NATO naval drills, which began June 5, and runs until June 20.

head Force, which NATO agreed to establish at the Wales NATO summit last September.

And they also discuss that these maneuvers will involve the expansion of the NATO response force, and some of the names of these maneuvers are: "Arctic Challenge," which involves eight countries and ended on Friday; "Steadfast Cobalt," which is mainly in Poland—this will go until the Fifteenth of June; another one in Holland; a series of so-called "Allied Shield" maneuvers in the Baltics, from the 5th to the 20th of June; "South Strike," from the 8th to the Nineteenth of June in Poland and the Baltics; "Noble Jump," 10th to the 21st of June in Poland and other locations; "Sea Breeze," from the 22nd of June to the 3rd of July, in the Black Sea; and "Trident Juncture," from the first of October to the 6th of November, in Italy, Portugal, and Spain.

And you simultaneously have Russian maneuvers, non-stop, matching the NATO maneuvers, including a maneuver of the Strategic Rocket Force last week. Last week you had the snap maneuvers in the Central Military District, and the message coming from all of that is very clear: that Russia is absolutely not going to back down.

A week ago, you had an incident where the *USS Ross*, which is an Aegis-equipped Ballistic Missile Defense destroyer, belonging to the Ballistic Missile Defense System, which the United States is building in Eastern Europe and in the Mediterranean, and that ship, the *USS Ross*, left the Romanian port of Constanta, moving toward Russian water. At that point, the Russian Navy sent SU-24 jets, and forced the *USS Ross* to turn around, and go back.

Now that incident is, or was, hair-raising, because there was, in the recent period, a whole bunch of top military experts from the United States and from Europe, who warned that, contrary to the Cold War and the Cuban Missile Crisis, today there is no red telephone between the President of the United States and that of Russia, and that the normal code of communication, the so-called red telephone, more or less, has completely broken down. And therefore, the danger of even an accidental launch, just some mistaken reading of screens, or some other human failure, could lead to launching of thermonuclear war, which at this point, would, in all likelihood, mean the extinction of civilization.

And the thing which is so horrifying about it, is that, during the Cuban Missile Crisis, when President Kennedy was in office, people were aware that nuclear war meant the annihilation of civilization; and compared to that time, we are now in a much, much more dangerous situation, for reasons I'm going to elaborate, than then, and there is no public debate! There is no mass protest! There is no peace movement in the streets.

In the middle-range missile crisis at the beginning of the 1980s, when the [Russian] SS-20 and the [U.S.] Pershing 2 were directed against each other, and all the time, at launch-on-warning, because the distance was so short, you had hundreds of thousands of people in street, in Europe, and people were aware how big the danger was. And now, everybody is sleepwalking, or watching TV, or going on vacation, or some other activity.

The U.S. First-Strike Policy

The growth of the NATO-U.S. missile defense system in Europe, when this started, it was clear to every military expert, that this meant that the United States had gone to a first-strike policy. And more recently, Russia denounced, in no uncertain terms, that they also regard the Prompt Global Strike doctrine as a first-strike doctrine.

The Russian Defense Ministry also was concerned

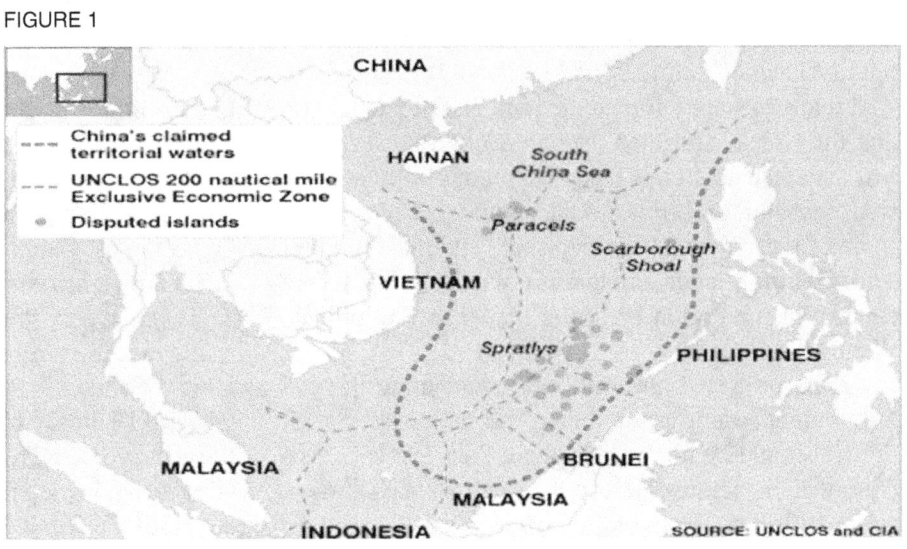

FIGURE 1

China's claimed territorial waters
--- UNCLOS 200 nautical mile Exclusive Economic Zone
◦ Disputed islands

CHINA · HAINAN · South China Sea · Paracels · Scarborough Shoal · VIETNAM · Spratlys · PHILIPPINES · MALAYSIA · BRUNEI · MALAYSIA · INDONESIA

SOURCE: UNCLOS and CIA

about an exercise in the Atlantic, with the involvement of eight countries, called RC Demonstration 2015, which simulates the interception of Russian ballistic missiles. And, over the Christmas period, President Putin already had announced the upgrade of the Russian military doctrine by saying that they regard these first-strike doctrines—the Ballistic Missile Defense System in Europe, and the Prompt Global Strike doctrine—as a severe security threat to the existence of Russia, and therefore, they preserve the right to even use nuclear weapons to prevent such a strategy from being successful.

Now that shows you in what proximity of the catastrophe we are.

The military leaders of Europe, with whom we are in contact, have assured us—and I don't want to name any names, but these are people who are really top, top experts—that all of these maneuvers, and all of these permanent rotations of U.S. troops to the Baltics, sending in tank battalions and other heavy equipment, all is just confetti. It doesn't mean anything. Because these troops could not possibly win a war against Russia in a conventional way. And this is just a PR campaign to calm the nerves of nervous Nellies in the Baltic countries who mostly have leaders who have been chosen in exile, and put in these positions.

But below the nuclear threshold, nothing would function. So we are not really talking about some conventional little war in Europe, but they are talking clearly about a thermonuclear war.

Exactly the same escalation of the confrontation is happening towards China right now (**Figure 1**). At the end of May, the U.S. Navy P-8A Poseidon surveillance aircraft flew over the Yongshu reef, which is part of Spratly Islands, and they had a CNN crew on board. And that CNN crew filmed the reef, and the people on this little rock, and then a tremendous PR campaign was launched about this being the proof of the "aggressive behavior of China." And naturally, China is on some of these rocks, filling up sand, and making them actually little islands, but that is not only China. Every country in the region has done that: The Philippines, Vietnam, and others.

China protested and said, this is violating the 12-mile radius around these reefs. And then Carter said, "There should be no mistake about this. The U.S. will fly, sail, and operate wherever international law allows, as we do around the world."

China Daily, at that point, rejected capitulation to U.S. bullying tactics, and said that this was just the U.S. implementing the pivot to Asia strategy, to counterbalance the rise of regional powers China and India. This was the first time they named India as being part of the reason why the United States is doing the Asia pivot policy.

Then the *Global Times*, the official Chinese paper, also said, experts warn of the potential of a military conflict over heightened U.S. surveillance over these islands, and a representative of the PLA Academy of Military Science, Peng Wanghang, said, "China will likely strike back if the U.S. comes within 12 miles of the islands. The U.S. is deliberately provoking China."

And what was the comment of the *Wall Street Journal*? "War on China Now." They say, "the longer the U.S. fails to contest Beijing's South China Sea claims, the more aggressive China will become, and perhaps willing to fight for them. The time to resist China's maritime pretensions is now."

Conflict in the South China Sea

Deng Xiaoping, already in the '80s, when little rumblings around these islands had come up, said, let's not fight over rocks in the South China Sea. Let's freeze the whole conflict. Let's jointly develop these places and benefit all of them, and leave it to future generations to figure out who has what territorial claim, but let's not get into fights right now.

That advice was obviously not taken, especially as the rise of China became an issue—and remember that [Chairman of the Joint Chiefs] General Dempsey repeatedly warned the West not to fall into the Thucydides

Trap over China, because the neo-cons, around the fall of the Soviet Union, had developed this idea that they would never allow *any* country to rise above the power and economic might of the United States, and not even a group of countries.

Now, China *is* rising. China is 1.4 billion people. India is probably 1.3 billion people, and they have high growth rates. China used to have a growth rate of up to 12%; now it has consciously reduced that to about 7%. India has a growth rate of 8%. So these countries are rising, and they represent many more people than the United States. So why should they not develop? But General Dempsey had warned the West not to fall into the Thucydides Trap, referring to Athens in ancient Greece, against Sparta, because when Sparta started to develop, the Athenians were worried that they would lose power, so they started the Peloponnesian War, and overstretched their empire, and that is how Classical Greece went under. So, Dempsey said, the United States should not make that mistake.

Obviously, they're not listening. And right now, you have all kinds of think-tanks—CSIS and others—who invite people from the South China region and have them play war games over these islands.

Already in 2012, Manila deployed its largest naval asset, a decommissioned U.S. 1960-era patrol cutter, to arrest Chinese fishermen on the Scarborough Shoal, there you see it (Figure 1), a reef in the northeast of the South China Sea. But then, it turned out the entrance was too small, and the water too shallow, for a warship, so instead they had to send a small boarding team, which went into the lagoon, and made the arrest. But that gave Chinese law enforcement enough time to send a vessel, and intervene. So Manila lost face because they were looking militaristic, sending a warship against fishermen, and having militarized the dispute.

China, at that point, retaliated with economic pressure, and for one full year, the Philippines had no ambassador to China, and eventually had to pick a new, more peaceful ambassador to assume that post.

Similarly, in 2012, China prevailed against Vietnam over disputed blue-water territories, and the Paracel's Woody Island. Now, the China Ministry of Foreign Affairs, Miss Hua Chunying, said in response that the Chinese land reclamations around the Meiji Reef, which is also claimed by the Philippines, only have the purpose of improving functions for the living conditions of the personnel who are stationed there, to help to develop maritime search-and-rescue disaster prevention, maritime science and research, meteorological observation, navigation, safety, fishery production service, and all kinds of civilian demands, in addition to military defense.

So, it is clear that the buildup of these reefs and shoals into artificial islands increases both thir civilian and the military use. But as the former Prime Minister of Australia Hawke just said, this is not a threat to anybody. Our ships are not being hampered, and they can travel through these areas without a problem.

Now, why should these rocks and a little sand on top of them, be such an issue, that people start talking about possible war between the United States and China?

Empire Politics

When I arrived in Beijing last February, in 2014, this was a few days before the Nazi coup in Kiev occurred. I was talking to Chinese officials, and I warned them that this could lead to a potential great war. And they had no idea. They were not interested in Ukraine. They said, oh, Ukraine is very far away, and we are much more concerned about our conflict with Japan and the South China Sea. Naturally that attitude has changed after the total escalation over Ukraine, but in Europe people have still a similar attitude. They say, oh, why discuss these rocks in the South China Sea? Why should we concern ourselves with this?

Well, both conflicts are the result of geopolitics, of empire politics, which led to two world wars already, so we should not dismiss such things at all. We have to go back to what geopolitics was before World War I, the crazy assumptions of such people as Mackinder and Milner, who. at that time, at the end of the Nineteenth Century, developed the idea that whoever controls the Eurasian mainland, is putting the Atlantic Rim countries at a disadvantage in terms of controlling the world.

At that point, you had in Europe and Eurasia, the Trans-Siberian Railroad developed. You had Bismarck, who adopted the American System of Economy, which was the idea coming from Henry C. Carey, the advisor of Lincoln, and these ideas were transmitted to Bismarck, especially by the head of the industrial association in Germany at the time, Wilhlem von Kardoff. The idea was that what generates wealth in society is not free trade; it's not the ability to buy cheap and sell dear, but it is entirely the development of the creative powers

Wikimedia Commons

The Trans-Siberian Railway in the Nineteenth Century.

of labor and the productive powers of industry.

Now, this adoption by Bismarck of the American System of Economy, as it was developed by Lincoln at the time, in a very short period of time, in a few years, turned Germany from a feudal country into one of the industrial powers of the world, and also, to have the best social system in the world, going along with that. But that was very much a thorn in the side of the British Empire at that point. Because if then, as in the '90s of the Nineteenth Century, the Trans-Siberian Railroad brought an advantage to trade via land, via railroad, they saw their control on the sea threatened.

So, the British did a whole bunch of maneuvers to derail this. One was, they used their influence in Germany to get the ouster of Bismarck [in 1890], which was really the beginning of World War I. They manipulated the landscape to have the Entente Cordiale, the Triple Entente, the attack by Japan on Russia in 1905, the two Balkan wars in 1912, and then, when the shots of Sarajevo occurred, this was just the trigger, but not the cause of this war.

World War I ended with the Versailles Treaty, and that Treaty had the seeds already of the Second World War, *and* the Third World War, if we don't stop it. At the end of World War I, the German-held territories of the Shandong Peninsula were transferred to Japan at the Paris Peace Conference in 1919. Shandong, including Jiaozhou and the Pacific Islands north of the equator, were supposed to go Japan. This included the Marshall

Islands, Micronesia, the Mariana Islands, and the Carolines. But Japan was very unhappy that only half of the rights of Germany were given to Japan, and they walked out of the conference.

The reason why Japan was treated so nicely—after all, they got half the territory—is because they had a secret agreement, in 1917, with Great Britain and France and Italy, that guaranteed these territories to Japan; and Japan, in turn, agreed that they would support the British annexing the Pacific islands south of the Equator. So Article 156 of the Treaty of Versailles transferred these German colonies and concessions in Jiaozhou, China, to Japan.

Naturally this led to the protest of Liu Tseng-Tsiang, head of the Chinese delegation, who rejected this agreement, and China, as a consequence, did not sign the treaty; it was the only country at that conference not to sign. China had a tremendous feeling of injustice and outrage, which led to the demonstrations which became known as the May 4 Movement. Thousands of students demonstrated in Beijing, in strikes and boycotts of Japanese goods—and also workers and merchants participated, and all layers of the society regarded the Versailles Treaty as an utter fraud.

John Foster Dulles, U.S. Secretary of State from 1953 to 1959.

Wikipedia.org

The San Francisco Peace Conference

Thirty years later, after the Second World War, there was the San Francisco peace conference, where China, thanks to John Foster Dulles, was not even seated. They were not even invited to participate, despite the fact that they had fought the Japanese longer than anybody, and they had the highest casualty rate in Asia.

So, the Western

The misnamed Versailles "peace" conference, June 28, 1919.

australianwarmemorial.gov.au

powers established the current Eastern Asian order in China's absence. And John Foster Dulles, who was the designer of the Treaty, deliberately left certain Asian frontier territories without owners. There is a book called the *The Cold War Frontiers in the Asia-Pacific*, written by Kimie Hara, which said that the San Francisco Peace Treaty created the causes for almost every subsequent territorial dispute in Asia. And this is a very long list of disputes: the Kurile Islands, the Northern Territory, the division of North and South Korea, the Dokto-Takashima Islands, the Senkaku-Diaoyu Islands, the separation of Taiwan from the Mainland, the Paracels-Yisha. which was that, and the Spratly Namsha islands.

This is why these conflicts can be activated every time you want to have a war. And it is obvious that you do not find the dynamics if you just look at the current-day media. And as I will show you in a second, the Ukraine crisis, and the conflict with Russia, come exactly from the same origin.

Now, the Versailles Treaty was not a peace treaty. It was a debt dungeon established in the interests of the financial oligarchy. No serious historian any more would claim that Germany was the only war party in the First World War, but as I said, this had a 30-year prehistory, where the main manipulators were really the British, for reasons that they hated the German industrial revolution introduced by Bismarck, and they hated the idea of the Eurasian development.

Nevertheless, the Versailles powers ruled that Germany had to pay both its own war debt, which was significant, and reparations. And that was so much more than German industry could possibly produce, that it led to the 1923 hyperinflation, the 1929 crash, the Great Depression of the '30s, and that all gave rise to the National Socialists [Nazis], and that way, the preparation for World War II was created.

The same method, by the way, was behind the 1916 Sykes-Picot agreement, which divided the Middle East in such a way that you could manipulate any ethnic situation whenever you wanted to. It also was the basis of the 1919 Trianon Treaty, which created the same kind of powder keg for the Balkans, and in each of these situations, potential future territorial conflicts were already built in.

Now, the same debt prison which Versailles meant to Germany after the First World War, which was really the seed of the catastrophe to come, has been imposed, for exactly the same reason, with the Maastricht Treaty, on all of Europe, and has led to the Ukraine crisis. Helmut Schmidt, the former Chancellor of Germany, whom you can disagree with on some points, but he was one of three German individuals in the last week— Helmut Schmidt, Gerhard Schröder, and Frank-Walter Steinmeier—who strongly came out against the confrontation with Russia, and strongly criticized Merkel for not inviting Putin to the G7 summit which takes place this weekend. Because none of the big conflicts, they argue, can be solved without Russia—not terrorism, not ISIS, not the Ukraine issue, not the financial crisis—so why not invite Putin to participate?

Now, Helmut Schmidt also said that the origin of the Ukraine crisis was the 1992 adoption of the Maastricht Treaty. Why? Because it was at that point that not only was a debt regime imposed over all of Europe, forbidding, for example, credit generation for productive purposes, but especially—and that is the argument Schmidt made—it was the beginning of the eastward expansion of the EU, which always went in parallel with the eastward expansion of NATO.

The Greek Debt Powderkeg

Now, the policy of the Troika against Greece—the Troika being the IMF, the European Central Bank, and the EU Commission—was to impose several "rescue packages" on Greece, which now has led to a complete debt of €360 billion. Ninety-seven percent of that money *never* remained in Greece, but immediately went back to pay the European banks, and only 3% of it stayed in Greece, so the Greek government has argued, legitimately, and understandably, that they cannot and will not pay that debt, because if you look the smallness

Creative Commons/OleReissmann

Former German Chancellor Helmut Schmidt.

of Greece, the smallness of the Greek economy, they would have to have a 200% growth rate of GDP in order to pay their debts. So they have demanded a debt-cancellation conference.

Five months of negotiations between the new Syriza-Independent Greeks government with the Troika have led to a complete standstill, and Greece was supposed to pay €300 million to the IMF on Friday. And then they were on the telephone with Merkel, with Hollande, and were presented with the ultimate list of tax increases by €3.5 billion, by more cuts in the pensions, in the health system—so, Prime Minister Tsipras said, this is unacceptable. This cannot be the basis for an agreement, because we have a red line, and that is we made promises to our population, and we won the election on that basis—that we will not pay debt which we regard as illegitimate.

Greece has, for the time being, said they will pay all the monies which will come due in June, which is, altogether, €1.5 billion by the end of June. That may be the beginning of the end, not only of the euro, but of the entire trans-Atlantic financial system. Because on this Greek debt, hangs several *trillion* in derivatives, and therefore, I think Tsipras has, for sure, the better cards, because [Finance Minister] Varoufakis is an economist, he knows his business, and they know perfectly well, that the moment the Eurozone kicks out Greece in an uncontrolled way, then you will have the evaporation of the entire trans-Atlantic financial system. And there is a swap agreement between the ECB and the Federal Re-

FIGURE 2
South America: Proposed Transcontinental Railroad Network

South America: Topography

EIRNS

Road of China in September, in Kazakhstan, in 2013, and especially the strengthening of the alliance among the BRICS countries [Brazil, Russia, India, China, South Africa] at the Fortaleza summit in July 2014 in Brazil, you have a completely new dynamic in the world. What has emerged—pretty much unknown to people in Europe and the United States, because the mass media have slandered this, or blacked it out completely—is a parallel economic and financial system. And in the last year alone, you have an unbelievable number of joint projects in infrastructure, scientific and technological cooperation, nuclear cooperation, joint space programs.

Infrastructure projects, for example, include the building of a second Panama Canal in Nicaragua, with the help of China. You had the visit of Prime Minister Li Keqiang in Brazil, Peru, and Chile, which resulted in a Memorandum of Understanding among China, Brazil, and Peru, to build a transcontinental railroad, which, for the first time in history, will unite the Pacific Ocean with the Atlantic Ocean by railway.

This is historic, because if you look at the map of Latin America, (**Figure 2**) up to now, you have *no* continent-wide infrastructure project, or system; you only have little pieces of railway from the raw materials to the port, which is the leftover from the colonial exploitation of Latin America. But this is now changing, because Li Keqiang went on to Chile, and they agreed to build four tunnels between Chile and Argentina, to also connect the trade, to have access to the Atlantic and the Pacific.

And this is all based on Xi Jinping's pronouncement to have a "win-win" policy—that naturally, China has advantages, it has expanding export markets—but it brings the urgently required infrastructure to these countries.

The BRICS have also agreed to create a completely new parallel financial system. The United States tried to

serve; therefore, they hang together; they have an outstanding derivatives debt exposure of $2 quadrillion.

So this is why you have right now the reemergence of this same geopolitical impulse, where some of the financial oligarchy just say—not everybody, because some of them have changed—some of them say: Well, if Asia is rising and the trans-Atlantic sector is collapsing, it is better that we risk a thermonuclear showdown, rather than letting them win this game.

The BRICS New Paradigm

That is why we are on the verge of World War III.

But it is not so simple anymore, because, in the meantime, a dramatic, dramatic change has occurred: Since Xi Jinping announced the policy of the New Silk

FIGURE 3

prevent anybody from joining the Asian Infrastructure Investment Bank, the AIIB, but then, Great Britain wanted to join, and then Germany, France, Italy, Scandinavia, Australia, Israel! So altogether, 58 nations wanted to become *founding* member-nations of the AIIB. And this bank, like all the other banks which I will name in a second, are not to speculate: They are only there to issue credit for infrastructure for the real economy.

The BRICS countries are bringing the New Development Bank into operation this coming July, around the BRICS summit in Ufa, Russia. And also, the Shanghai Cooperation Organization, which has its summit at that time in Ufa, will have their own development bank; the SAARC countries, this is the South Asian Association for Regional Cooperation, will have their own development bank; China has created, in addition, a New Silk Road Development Fund, a Maritime Silk Road Fund. And so this is really taking off.

All of these banks have around $100 billion core capital—naturally, they can lend out much more money than their basic capital; the BRICS have also created a Contingent Reserve Arrangement, which is a pool to defend all participating countries against speculative attacks. They have learned their lesson from the Asia crisis [1997-98], when such people as George Soros, speculated the currencies of Asia down by 80% *in one week* in '97!

This has been going on, especially in the last year. There is a completely new economic and financial system emerging, and as I said, the media did not report it at all. Instead, they had slanders against Xi Jinping,

Putin, naturally, the "demon"; Xi Jinping, the new "dictator" and Mao Zedong, "tensions between China and India." So they're only reporting things which were either outright lies, or negative images, so that people in America or Europe would not know about these positive developments.

A Glimpse of Reality Emerges

But this is now changing: Over the last two, three weeks, the success of this new system is becoming so overwhelming that the media could not help but to report about it. This is *Time* magazine, with the headline, "New Silk Road Could Change Global Economics Forever" (**Figure 3**). This is written by Robert Berke, and it goes through all of these projects, going into the history of the ancient Silk Road, Marco Polo, but especially coming to the present situation. But then, it still has the spin, by saying, "all this is, is really a chess game for the control of Eurasia. This will lead to a new Cold War, where the outcome is still completely open."

This is another such article, "Could the New Silk Road End Geopolitical Tensions?"

And then also, there is lengthy reportage on the official German radio Deutschlandfunk: "China's New Silk Road: Old Route, New Ways," also going into the legendary ancient Silk Road in great detail, actually quite excitedly reporting that this is really taking off, with *huge* development projects. But then, they say, you know, the Chinese propaganda is that this is for the benefit for all of mankind—which gets them very upset, and they don't want to believe it.

And they say, "Ja, there is the one route which goes

from the ancient emperor's city of Xi'an, through Central Asia to Russia, Poland, and ends in the city of Duisburg—Duisburg is the largest interior port of Europe, where Xi Jinping went, when he recently went to Germany, and they received him with the big banner, "The Silk Road Has Arrived in Germany." But then they say there is also a second route, which goes from the ancient city of Kashgar, which is in the west of China, all the way to Kyrgyzstan, Uzbekistan, Iran, Turkey, and also ends up in Europe. And, it involves the famous Karakorum Highway going from Kashgar to Pakistan, and so forth and so on.

A couple of months ago, I had requested at a conference similar to this, that we absolutely must get a public debate, in Europe and in the United States, about the fact that an alternative to a collapsing trans-Atlantic system exists, and that China and the BRICS countries have offered to the West to cooperate and be part of it. And I would say it is a certain success of our work that we have now several major articles reporting that. And I'm only picking out a couple. Also, the director of International Security Studies at the British Royal United Services Institute [RUSI], which is the leading military think-tank of the U.K., Raffaello Pantucci, said this dynamic cannot be stopped; it will happen anyway. The Chinese Silk Road *is* the way out for the European crisis. Why not just cooperate?

The Carnegie Tsinghua Center for Global Policy also said that this is the chance for Greece to recover the lost economic space of the past 20 years, and become an advanced country, cooperating with the BRICS and the Silk Road. And that is actually the position of the Greek government, which has said, for a long time, that Greece, which has historical, long traditional ties with China—they pride themselves that when China had the Silk Road, and even before that, an ancient civilization, Greece was one of the cradles, or *the* cradle of European civilization, and they had, through the ancient Silk Road, deep cultural and economic ties; and therefore, Greece should revive now the bridge between Europe and China. And Greece, because of the Orthodox Church and other historical ties, has also extremely good relations with Russia.

Also an economist from Ecuador, Pedro Páez, asked, why is Europe not just cooperating with the Silk Road? The austerity drive has no future, it failed in Latin America before, and it will fail in Europe, while the Silk Road represents the hope for Europe to revive its economy.

theepochtimes.com

A statue of Confucius in Beijing in 2008 (detail).

Confucius and the Mandate of Heaven

Now, how should we look at that? China is preparing a completely different model of government and of relations among states. I can only encourage you to read a book which contains 70 of the recent speeches of Xi Jinping from 2013-14, called *The Governance of China*, because if you read these 70 speeches, you get a sense that you have a *completely* different leader in front of you, than we are accustomed to in the West, since the murder of the John F. Kennedy, or the ouster of Adenauer and de Gaulle. Because we have more or less dwarves as political leaders who are involved in scandals, who are involved in all kinds of things, but who have not presented a vision.

As a matter of fact, I can tell you, in Europe right now, we have a lot of people who say, all our governments are doing is crisis management; they were running and panting after one crisis after the other, like a dog exhausted from a long run, but they have no vision, they have no solutions, and that is why what is offered here is so attractive.

One quote from Xi Jinping: "We had an obligation to fulfill a dream for humanity. Instead of working against each other, we must work together as states. For that we need trust and unity. We have to name the old ways as inappropriate for the 21st Century. Each country is like a little light, but if we bring them together, we can light up the night sky."

The key to understanding China is Confucius, because Confucianism was the official state philosophy of China for about 2,500 years, with only the very short interruption of the Cultural Revolution, but it is practically in the genes of all Chinese.

Xi Jinping talks about the "Chinese dream" and the

"dream for humanity." This actually comes from this Confucian conception of how society should be organized. In the center of this philosophy, is the idea of the perfectibility of man, that you cannot govern a country only by legislation or decrees, or by punishment. He says, if a people is regulated only through the threat of punishment and decrees, it may be possible to get them not to do what is forbidden, but they will not develop a feeling of shamefulness. (Now that somehow sounds familiar, if you look at the present.) But if people are guided by morality and ethical customs, he says, they will not only develop shamefulness, but they will be striving for perfectibility.

Confucius developed his philosophy against a long period of war and chaos in China, and he proceeded from the idea that there is a higher lawfulness in the universe, than that which guides the political activities of the day. He called that, like other philosophers before him, the "Mandate of Heaven." This is an idea which, in European philosophy, appeared as the notion of "natural law," that there is an in-built, higher lawfulness, which man can violate, for a little bit, but sooner or later, these higher laws will punish the violators. And in the same way, Confucius says that the Mandate of Heaven, which means the obligation to create an harmonious development of society—and harmony means not just peace or calmness—it means, consensus of the governed, unity, and all of this directed toward the common progress in society.

The closest thinker in European philosophy I have found who matches the ideas of Confucius, is the famous scientist Nicholas of Cusa, of the Fifteenth Century, who not only was the father of modern science in Europe and therefore, also America, but also the creator of a sovereign republic, the idea of the modern nation-state. He developed, for the first time, the idea that rulership must be based on the consensus of the governed, and that is exactly the idea of Confucius, who says the government must act on the Mandate of Heaven, and if the government is bad and loses that mandate, it is the obligation of *Chun-Tzu*, the "noble sages," to replace that government and bring the state back into order.

Nicholas of Cusa had the idea that government not only should be provided by the wisest, but those of the wisest who have the strongest sense of lawfulness, for the legality of the state. Now, what the mandate is, is an objective matter: It's natural law, it's a high order within

FIGURE 4

This depiction of Cardinal Nicholas of Cusa (in the red robe) is a detail of the altar piece at his private chapel in Bernkastel Kues. The painter was Matthias Grünewald (1470-1528).

Creation. But to recognize that, and to act on it, requires the development of humanity. Therefore, Confucius put so much emphasis on education, especially to develop virtue.

The educational method which Confucius developed is not based on teaching facts or giving information, but by inspiration, by being a role model, and the aim is the search for truth. And Confucius even had the idea to throw his pupils periodically into a crisis, so that they would find a deeper and better truth, and be willing to take down their previous assumptions.

Confucian 'Aesthetics'

In that sense, Confucian ideas are also very similar to the idea of the "aesthetical education" of Friedrich Schiller, which is still, in my view, the most noble idea, namely that one is able to educate every human being to become a beautiful soul and a genius.

Now, Nicholas of Cusa developed a method of thinking in the *De Docta Ignorantia*—this is actually a very nice picture (**Figure 4**). When you go to Bernkastel-Kues the next time (which you should do pretty soon), because that's the birthplace of Nicholas of Cusa, and you see this painting in the little chapel in the hospital which he donated 500 years ago, and which is still in operation for about 35 people, as an old people's home. There's a little chapel, and it has this painting and another one, in which you see the bad clergy who go to Hell. So, since he was a key reformer of the Church and would have made Luther completely superfluous, I find it quite interesting that he had such an idea.

In one of his main writings, *De Docta Ignorantia*, or *On Learned Ignorance*, Cusa has this idea that man never knows the truth, but is in a perfect process of perfection and self-perfection; Confucius says more or less the same thing. He says: A good man does not slavishly follow the steps of others. He's not even following slavishly his own steps, because experience has taught him that every occasion is different, and you have to permanently evaluate each situation afresh, and then choose what is the next step.

Confucius also was very strongly of the opinion that Classical music elevates man, while destructive music destroys society. Now, if you look at the music of the Atlantic region today, I think we should be extremely worried. And he says, the effect of bad music has the same negative effect as populist orators; these people know how to talk very well, but only to achieve a sudden effect to please a sensuous experience of the audience, but watch out; these people are always only following their own interests and therefore are very dangerous.

Nicholas of Cusa has the same polemic against the school of rhetoric which, during his time, was very popular among the Scholastics, and they were based on the Aristotelian school of rhetoric, in which you just have to learn to talk up your issues well, and then you will have success. I would say that almost every politician in the United States and Europe right now, at best, are well-trained rhetorical orators, and therefore, they are very dangerous.

I think if you look at all of this, there is no question in my mind, and I hope to at least make you curious enough that you investigate it on your own, that Xi Jinping is a completely Confucian man. He said *The Governance of China*:

"People make history and work creates the future. Work is the fundamental force, driving the progress in society. Happiness does not fall from the sky, nor dreams become true automatically, but through work. Work is industrious, honest, creative. Work is the most honorable, sublime, magnificent, and beautiful. It releases the creative potential and it creates a better future

Xinhua/Huang Jingwen
China's President Xi Jinping addresses an international seminar marking the 2,565th birthday of Confucius, Sept. 24, 2014.

for all. Innovation is the soul of a nation's progress. Science and technology are the primary productive forces. This is why China is training such a large number of high-caliber creative scientists and engineers. We are proud of having the most scientists and engineers in the whole world."

He also said that they want to replace, as quickly as possible, the mark "Made in China," with "Created, Invented in China." The Chinese dream is to create a better future for the whole society, based on the fullest development of the creative potential of every individual in society. The New Silk Road policy offers that participation in that in a "win-win" policy: Everybody can participate and replicate the Chinese dream, which has led to the astounding economic miracle of China, in which China developed in 30 years, what Europe and the United States took almost 200 years to accomplish.

President Xi offered to President Obama at the APEC conference last October in Beijing, a new model of relations between major countries, which is based on mutual respect for each other's sovereignty, non-interference in the internal affairs; respect for the different social systems; and, based on a "win-win" cooperation—which happens to be the same principle as the Peace of Westphalia which ended the Thirty Years War in Europe, which established that foreign policy must be based on the interest of the other. That happens to be also the basis of international law, and the UN Charter.

Revive the American Dream

Now, how should we, and how can we, therefore, overcome the *immediate* danger of thermonuclear war, *and* the immediate danger that this beautiful mankind would *vanish* in extinction! Well, I think it's very simple: What we have to do, and especially what you have to do, is to revive the American dream. Remember that such a thing once existed? The dream of the Founding Fathers was to create a republic, to make this country a "beacon of hope and a temple of liberty," where every person from around the globe would be happy to come to and become an American. The idea of a republic, of a constitution, which was based on the principles of the common good, and the non-violation of sovereignty, not only for the present but also for future generations.

How can we overcome the danger of a financial blowout? Well, it's very simple: We have to end the casino economy which is driving the war. How do we do that? Implement Glass-Steagall. Now, fortunately, the Presidential campaign of Martin O'Malley is taking prominence more and more every day, and he has said that the first action he would take when he gets into the White House, would be to implement Glass-Steagall: Now that would mean ending this high-profit maximizing of the profit of a few, and going back to the American System of Economy. It should not be surprising that the *Wall Street Journal* therefore, has declared Martin O'Malley "enemy number-one" in an article yesterday, and O'Malley said he is proud of that.

Therefore, it is the task of every patriotic American to help Lyndon LaRouche, to help us, and to help, in general, to create a team around O'Malley, which can revive every aspect of the republican tradition of America, especially the policies of Alexander Hamilton, who, after all, created a National Bank, he unified the country by taking over the debt of the different states, which was $70 million at the time, an astronomical figure, and he created then a credit system based on his four reports to the Congress. And all of this had the same idea: that the only source of wealth *is* the creative ability of the population.

So all the United States has to do to cooperate with the AIIB, the New Development Bank, the BRICS, the New Silk Road, is go back to your own tradition, go back to the principles of the American Revolution. The United States must be pushed to take up the offer of Xi Jinping, and to cooperate in the great projects! And that means, not only create projects in Asia, Latin America, and Africa: but rebuild the United States! I think if you have travelled some of the roads between Washington and New York recently, I think you should be convinced that you need infrastructure! Have you traveled on the Amtrak? You need a high-speed train system!

Therefore, reviving the American dream would mean, to build a fast train system, preferably a maglev system or some other technology, from the North to the South, from the East to the West; not have the Amtrak system, in which people die because of a lack of safety, and Cass Sunstein's policies of a couple of years ago; but have the idea that we could build, in the United States, 30, 40, 50,000 km of fast train! You would stop having these old and not so secure airplanes for travel on the East Coast. You would have a fast train, a maglev system, where the travel time would be a quarter of what it is now by plane, because you would just get into the station, you would travel an hour, and you are already in Chicago or someplace else.

And that's just the beginning of the technologies which are now being developed further by the Chinese, to be able to travel at the speed of 1,000 miles an hour in the near future.

Now, why not rebuild America? America needs new cities! India is building *100 new cities*, so-called "smart cities." These are cities which do not have your typical suburban sprawl and then some strip malls with Dunkin' Donuts, and then McDonalds and then—. And it doesn't matter where you go, in each city, it's the same. If you are dropped by helicopter, into one of these strip malls, you don't know where you are, because they are each exactly the same in every place in the United States!

Let's build *beautiful* cities! Let's build smart cities, where all the infrastructure is put underground, a modular system, in which the sewerage, the water, the electricity, the transport, is underground, and then, have the core of the city be new universities, libraries, theaters, operas, research facilities; then build housing around that; let the population participate in urban culture, which is lacking today.

New York is probably the only city—maybe Chicago and maybe Boston, a little bit—but you need urban culture! Why is it that China has the most Classical musicians in the world—the most vocalists and most instrumentalists? Because they know that Classical music is what makes creativity easy.

And let's declare a war against the drought! Right now large parts of America—California, Texas, and other states west of the Mississippi—are being lost! And because you have greenie politicians who say, there must be "water conservation," you know, water use is being reduced by Jerry Brown in California, by 25%, or even 35%, and that destroys agriculture, it destroys cities, it destroys human living conditions for people.

Let's declare a war on the drought: California is located on the ocean, so there is enough water. Let's build a couple of small nuclear plants to desalinate large amount of ocean water. Let's revive NAWAPA, bring the water which is now flowing into the Arctic in Canada and in Alaska, down along the Rocky Mountains, through a system of canals, all the way to Mexico: Which was already being discussed in Congress during the time of John F. Kennedy. Let's apply the knowledge we have about cosmic radiation and the processes in the galaxy to have ionization of moisture over the ocean, let's have cloud formation, change the rain patterns, reclaim the deserts in the Southwest of the United States.

Let's have a revival of the American Dream. There is no reason why people should forget what that was. Let's create a mass movement for development. And let's go back to the foreign policy of John Quincy Adams. Let's create an alliance of sovereign nation-states, working together for the common aims of mankind, and realize the dream for all of humanity.

It is so clear, that if we don't change our ways now, if we don't go to a completely new paradigm, we may not exist by the end of this year. But a new paradigm, a new epoch of human civilization, which would realize the idea that the human species is the only creative species known so far in the universe, means also that this humanity is too precious, too beautiful, too lovable, to be risked in thermonuclear war.

Let's turn the United States around, and accept the "win-win" perspective. And let me give you one thought for you to think about: Can you imagine the joy around the world—which now is not so fond of the United States; due to two Bushes, Obama, and the image of the United States has become the lowest around the world—if the United States would now turn around and say, "we are participating in this new paradigm"? The whole world would be so happy, and it is *absolutely possible*.

So I really ask you, work with us to accomplish that.